D1451000

APARTHEID

GARLAND REFERENCE LIBRARY
OF SOCIAL SCIENCE
(VOL. 587)

APARTHEID
A Selective Annotated Bibliography, 1979–1987

Sherman E. Pyatt

GARLAND PUBLISHING, INC. • NEW YORK & LONDON
1990

Library of Congress Cataloging-in-Publication Data

Pyatt, Sherman E.
  Apartheid : a selective annotated bibliography, 1979–1987 /
Sherman E. Pyatt.
    p. cm. — (Garland reference library of social science ; vol.
587)
    Includes index.
    ISBN 0–8240–7637–0 (alk. paper)
    1. Apartheid—South Africa—Bibliography. 2. South Africa—Race
relations—Bibliography. I. Title. II. Series: Garland reference
library of social science ; v. 587.
Z3608.R3P93 1990
[DT763]
016.3058'00968—dc20   89–7710
                                                                     CIP

Printed on acid-free, 250-year-life paper
Manufactured in the United States of America

DEDICATED TO

Shomari, Sean, Marilyn, Loretta,

and

Uncle Melvin

CONTENTS

PREFACE

The system of apartheid has a long history in South Africa. Make no mistake about it, racial discrimination is not a recent phenomenon in that country. Its roots stem from the 17th century when the descendants of the Dutch settlers, now known as Afrikaners, arrived on the southern tip of Africa. An example of a problem with race can be observed as early as 1652 when Jan van Riebeeck landed with a group of whites at the Cape of Good Hope. There they encountered a number of African tribes. The whites proceeded to establish a separate colony on the same land that the Africans regarded as theirs.

Webster's New Universal Unabridged Dictionary defines apartheid as "the policy of strict racial segregation and discrimination against the native Negroes and other colored peoples as practiced in South Africa." The word itself means separateness. The basic philosophy of apartheid is that each of the different groups or races in South Africa has a different (cultural) contribution to make to society and a unique destiny of its own. In essence, Afrikaners view apartheid as a means of maintaining their survival as a race of people.

Though the system of racial segregation was practiced in the very early beginnings of the Afrikaners' arrival in South Africa, the word apartheid was not used until 1948 by the National Party during the general election. From the time when the word was first used, there have been some changes and modifications to it.

ix

The word that is used these days, particularly by State President P.W. Botha, is "co-operative co-existence." Through this grew the idea of homelands and blacks having political independence. The underlying truth of the matter was that non-European people, especially blacks, were and are being discriminated against.

Another example of early race problems developing in South Africa is demonstrated by the first so-called Immorality Act in 1865. This law prohibited sexual intercourse and marriage between full-blooded blacks and whites.

Opponents of apartheid claim that no matter how much you change the name or make superficial adjustments to the constitution it is still a system structured to keep the economic and political power in the hands of the whites at any expense. Supporters give many reasons for their belief that the policy is good for South Africa.

There is no doubt that this system is deeply entrenched in the hearts and minds of all South Africans. It seems that it will take just as much time to dismantle apartheid as it did to set the foundation for it.

Since nothing stays the same, there will be a change in South Africa's system of apartheid. When this change will come and what type of change it will be are the questions that laymen and experts alike have been and are still trying to answer.

There is a wealth of information available on the subject of South Africa and an even greater amount on the topic of the system of apartheid. This topic has generated a great deal of attention and will continue to be a major issue for quite some time. Students and researchers are constantly in search of information concerning some aspect of apartheid; however, I have found that there are no concise research tools that allow the scholars, researchers, or students the opportunity to find such information.

The main purpose of this work is to explore the effects of apartheid on the people of South Africa and its indirect effect on the world. I have chosen to do this through the use of bibliographic citations of materials covering monographs, articles, and U.S. and U.N. documents.

Moreover, I have concentrated on material that covers the time that Reagan and Botha came into power in their respective countries, which would be between 1979 and 1980. The purpose of including this material is to examine whether there was any change in ideology or policy by the United States government regarding apartheid.

The material listed in this work dates from 1979 to the present. An earlier book, Index to Literature on Race Relations in South Africa, 1910 to 1975, by P. Potgieter, G.K. Hall 1979, touches upon some of the areas that I concentrate on in this bibliography.

My work updates the 1979 work by Potgieter and provides a broader and more in-depth coverage of the material on this subject.

Chapter 1 contains information on the origin of apartheid and how the system developed.

Chapter 2 details how the effects of the system of apartheid have influenced the economic and labor conditions of South Africa.

Chapter 3 examines the government's role in carrying out the laws of racial segregation and considers how this system has influenced politics as well.

Chapter 4 includes material on the living conditions and the general way of life of the people of South Africa.

Chapter 5 pertains to that country's dual educational system, from primary to higher education.

Chapter 6 includes material about the different ideologies of the churches in South Africa and how they interpret the system of apartheid.

Chapter 7 pertains to the various ideologies of other countries around the world and to individuals outside of South Africa regarding how they view apartheid.

Chapter 8 includes information on the various groups and organizations in South Africa that are seeking to bring an end to the system of apartheid.

Each of the chapters, except chapters 1 and 6, is subdivided into monographs, articles, and U.S. and U.N. documents; omitted are the numerous newspaper articles and foreign publications.

Brief annotations are provided to assist the user in making selections. Some citations appear without annotations if the source was not personally examined or if the title is self-explanatory.

Included are author and subject indexes and an appendix of the major laws and regulations relating to the policy of racial segregation in South Africa.

ACKNOWLEDGMENTS

I would like to acknowledge a few who gave me encouragement and advice. Many thanks to the entire Daniel Library staff, Marion, Pearl, and Barbara, thanks a million. Thanks to my cohorts: Cal, Jerry, Billy, Ellsworth, Ron, Roy, Tony, and their wives. Also, I would like to extend my deep appreciation to Quonset, Elise, Roslyn, Loretta, K.B. and Jackie. My very special thanks goes to Janie Dingle for typing and correcting this work and to Gail Tolbert for the initial and final proofreading. Ladies, I am indebted to you.

I am especially indebted to the Citadel Development Foundation for making this project possible. Finally, special thanks to Marilyn, Sean, and Shomari for their patience and understanding throughout this entire project.

Although many people assisted and encouraged me in this endeavor, I take full responsibility for any omissions or errors that may appear in this work. It is my hope that this selective bibliography will serve as a valuable resource for those who seek to know more about the system of apartheid.

LIST OF ABBREVIATIONS

Afr Bus - African Business
Afr Communist - African Communist
Afr Cont Rec - Africa Contemporary Record
Afric Affairs - African Affairs
Africa Hist - Africa History
Africa Rep - Africa Report
Afr News - Africa News
Afr Today - Africa Today
AGB Rept - Association of Governing Boards Report
Akron Business and Economic Rev - Akron Business and
     Economic Review
Am Academy Pol Soc Science - American Academy of
     Political and Social Science
Am-Arab Affairs - American - Arab Affairs
Am J Econ Sociol - American Journal of Economics and
     Sociology
Am J Intl Law - American Journal of International Law
Am Spectator - American Spectator
Anthro Educ Q - Anthropology and Education Quarterly
Atl Mo - Atlantic Monthly
Aus For Affairs Rec - Australian Foreign Affairs Record
Aust Out - Australian Outlook

Beijing R - Beijing Review
Black Enterp - Black Enterprise
Black Sch - Black Scholar
Boston Col Internat and Comp Law R - Boston College
     International and Comparative Law Review
Boston Globe Mag - Boston Globe Magazine
Bull Atom Sci - Bulletin of the Atomic Scientists
Bus & Soc R - Business and Society Review
Bus Week - Business Week

Cal Manag R - California Management Review
Can J Afr Stud - Canadian Journal of African Studies
Can R Stud Natl - Canadian Review of Studies in
     Nationalism
Chr and Crisis - Christianity and Crisis
Chr Cent - Christian Century
Chris Sci Mon - Christian Science Monitor
Christ Tod - Christianity Today
Chron Higher Educ - Chronicle of Higher Education
Common Cause Mag - Common Cause Magazine
Comp E - Comparative Education
Comp Educ R - Comparative Education Review
Comp Stud Soc Hist - Comparative Studies in Society and
     History
Comt - Commentary
Comw - Commonwealth
Cong Dig - Congressional Digest
Cong Q - Congressional Quarterly
Cong Q W Rep - Congressional Quarterly Weekly Report
Contemp R - Contemporary Review
Curr Bib African Affairs - Current Bibliography of
     African Affairs
Curr Hist - Current History

DAI - Dissertation Abstracts International
Denver J Int L and Pol - Denver Journal of
     International Law and Policy
Dept State Bul - Department of State Bulletin
Dev and Peace - Development and Peace

Edit Res Rept - Editorial Research Reports
Educ Rec - Educational Record
Ethnic & Racial Stud - Ethnic & Racial Studies
Ethnic Stud - Ethnic Studies

For Affairs - Foreign Affairs
Foreign Pol - Foreign Policy
Found News - Foundation News
Free at Issue - Freedom at Issue

Govt Fin R - Government Finance Review

Harper - Harper's Magazine
Harv Bus - Harvard Business Review
Harv Educ R - Harvard Education Review
Harv Women's Law J - Harvard Women's Law Journal

Health/PAC Bull-Health/PAC Bulletin
Howard Law J - Howard Law Journal
Human Rights Q - Human Rights Quarterly

Ins Def Stud J - Institute of Defense Studies Journal
Intercollegiate R - Intercollegiate Review
Intercom - Intercommunication
Inter Educ - Integrated Education
Inter Labour - International Labour
Internat J World Peace - International Journal of World
    Peace
Internat Labour Repts - International Labour Reports
Inter Pr - Intercontinental Press
Intl Affairs - International Affairs
Intl Affairs Bull - International Affairs Bulletin
Intl Comm Jurist R - International Commission of Jurist
    Review
Intl Contem African Stud - International Contemporary
    African Studies
Intl Perspect - International Perspectives
Int Org - International Organization
Int Sec - Internatonal Security
Italy Docs and Notes - Italy. Documents and Notes

J African Stud - Journal of African Studies
J Asian African Stud - Journal of Asian African Studies
J Can Res - Journal of Canadian Research
J Confl Res - Journal of Conflict Resolution
J Contem Hist - Journal of Contemporary History
J Def Dipl - Journal of Defense Diplomacy
J Ethnic Stud - Journal of Ethnic Studies
J Int Aff - Journal of International Affairs
J Mod Afric Stud - Journal of Modern African Studies
J Negro Educ - Journal of Negro Education
J Soc and Pol Econ Stud - Journal of Social, Political,
    and Economic Studies
J Wld Trade Law - Journal of World Trade Law

Labour Res - Labour Research
Law and Pol Int Bus - Law and Policy in International
    Business

Macl Mag - Maclean's Magazine
Middle East R - Middle East Review
Midwest Q - Midwest Quarterly
Mo R - Monthly Review

Multi Bus - Multinational Business
Multinatl - Multinational Monitor

Nat Geog - National Geographic
Nat Interst - National Interest
Natl J - National Journal
Natl Rep - National Report
Nat R - National Review
New A - New African
New England J Med - New England Journal of Medicine
New Jersey Rep - New Jersey Report
New Repub - New Republic
New WR - New World Review
NY - New Yorker
NY Times M - New York Times Magazine
NY Univ Intl J Law Pol - New York University Journal of
     International Law and Politics

Pet Econ - Petroleum Economist
Policy R - Policy Review
Polit Aff - Political Affairs
Polit Sci Q - Political Science Quarterly
Pol Service R - Political Service Review
Pol Stud - Political Studies
Pub Opin - Public Opinion

R African Pol Econ - Review of African Political
     Economy
R Black Pol Econ - Review of Black Political Economy
Read Digest - Reader's Digest
R Internat Affairs - Review of International Affairs
R Intl Stud - Review of International Studies
R Radical Pol Econ - Review of Radical Political
     Economics

So Africa - Southern Africa
Soc Educ - Social Education
Soc Sci Rec - Social Science Record
Soc Work - Social Work
South Africa Found News - South Africa Foundation News
South Africa Intl - South Africa International
South Africa Intl Q - South Africa International
     Quarterly
South Africa R - South Africa Review
Sports Ill - Sports Illustrated

Stanford J Intl Law - Stanford Journal of
     International Law

Third World Q - Third World Quarterly
Thurg Marsh Law R - Thurgood Marshall Law Review
Times Educ Suppl - Times Educational Supplement
Times Higher Educ Suppl - Times Higher Education
     Supplement
Trans Afr Forum - Trans Africa Forum
Trusts & Es - Trusts and Estates

UN Chron - United Nations Chronicle
UN Mon Chron - United Nations Monthly Chronicle
US News World Rep - US News & World Report

Va J Intl L - Virginia Journal of International Law
Vital Speeches - Vital Speeches of the Day

Wash Post M - Washington Post Monthly
W Comp Pres Docs - Weekly Compilation of Presidential
     Documents
Wld Dev - World Development
Wld Pol J - World Policy Journal
Wld Press Rev - World Press Review
Wld Today - World Today
Work Papers for a New Soc - Working Papers for a New
     Society
Work Wom - Working Woman
World Marxist R - World Marxist Review

Yale R - Yale Review

Apartheid

APARTHEID: A GENERAL OVERVIEW

Monographs

1. Adams, Heribert. <u>South Africa Without Apartheid;</u>
   <u>Dismantling Racial Domination.</u> Berkeley,
   Calif.: Univ. of Calif. Press, 1986. 315 pp.

   Adams seeks to discover the reasons why
   apartheid has lasted so long, how it will be
   abolished, and what kinds of government and race
   relations will evolve from this system.

2. Aeschliman, Gordon D. <u>Apartheid: Tragedy in Black</u>
   <u>and White</u>. Ventura: Regal Books, 1986, 178
   pp.

   Aeschliman, a native South African, asks
   several questions about the country's ability to
   avoid a Communist takeover, and what role the
   church plays in carrying out the system of
   apartheid.

3. <u>Apartheid: The Facts.</u> London: International
   Defense and Aid Fund for Southern Africa,
   1983. 112 pp.

4. Bigelow, William. <u>Strangers in Their Own Country:</u>
   <u>A Curriculum Guide on South Africa.</u> Trenton:
   Africa World Press, 1985. 92 pp.

   Bigelow's curriculum guide for high schools
   gives an overview of the effects apartheid has on
   blacks and other minorities in Africa.

5.   Brown, Godfrey N. Apartheid: A Teacher's Guide.
     Paris: UNESCO Press, 1981.   104 pp.

     Part of this work involves presenting
     essential facts concerning apartheid and its
     effects, and national and international efforts to
     eliminate the system of racial discrimination.

6.   Cell, John W. The Highest Stage of White
     Supremacy: The Origins of Segregation in
     South Africa and the American South. New
     York: Cambridge University Press, 1982.   320
     pp.

7.   Cooper, Carol. Survey of Race Relations in South
     Africa, 1983. New York: South African
     Institute of Race Relations, 1984.   700 pp.

8.   Davies, Robert H. The Struggle for South Africa:
     A Reference Guide to Movements,
     Organizations, and Institutions. London:
     Zed Books, 1984.   256 pp. Vol. I.

     In Chapter 1, the author talks about the
     origin and historical development of apartheid.

9.   Gordimer, Nadine. Lifetimes: Under Apartheid.
     New York: Knopf, 1986.   115 pp.

     The author combines excerpts from short
     stories along with photographs of life for blacks
     in South Africa.

10. Gordon, Loraine, ed. Survey of Race Relations in
     South Africa 1979. Johannesburg: South
     African Institute of Race Relations, 1980.

11. Gutteridge, William. <u>South Africa: Evolution or Revolution?</u> London: Institute for the Study of Conflict, 1984. 38 pp.

12. Hellman, Ellen, and Lever, Henry, eds. <u>Race Relations in South Africa 1929-1979.</u> New York: St. Martin's Press, 1979.

13. Hill, Christopher R. <u>Change in South Africa: Blind Alleys or New Directions?</u> Totowa, New Jersey: Barnes and Noble, 1983. 224 pp.

13a. James, Wilmot G., ed. <u>The State of Apartheid.</u> Boulder, Colo.: L. Rienner, 1986.

The author examines the content and length of debate among blacks and whites in South Africa on the topic of race relations.

14. Lambley, Peter. <u>The Psychology of Apartheid.</u> Athens: University of Georgia Press, 1980. 291 pp.

Lambley observes the origin and rise of apartheid in South Africa and the effects of this system on the people of that country.

15. Lapping, Brian. <u>Apartheid: A History.</u> New York: G. Braziller, 1986.

The author gives an in-depth overview of the origin of the system of apartheid.

16. Omitted.

17. Myers, Desaix, III. "Background: The Development and Context of Apartheid." Chapter 1 in <u>U.S. Business in South Africa: The Economic, Political and Moral Issues.</u> Bloomington: Indiana University Press, 1980.

Examines the historical perspective of the system of racial inequality.

18. Mzimela, Sipo E. Apartheid: South African Nazism.
    New York: Vantage, 1983. 245 pp.

         Mzimela states, "We must compare what is
    happening in South Africa under apartheid with
    what happened in Nazi Germany. We must examine
    whether there is any connection between the roles
    played by the Western governments, the
    transnational corporations, and the Western Church
    in apartheid in South Africa and the roles they
    played in Nazi Germany."

19. Randal, Peter, ed. Survey of Race Relations in
    South Africa, 1982. New York: South African
    Institute of Race Relations, 1983. 650 pp.

20. Rex, John, ed. Apartheid and Social Research.
    Paris: UNESCO, 1981. 199 pp.

21. Simson, Howard. Social Origins of Afrikaan
    Fascism and Its Apartheid Policy. Stockholm:
    Almqvist & Wiksell Inter., 1980.

22. This is Apartheid: A Pictorial Introduction.
    London: International Defense and Aid Fund
    for Southern Africa, 1984. 40 pp.

23. Uhlig, Mark A., ed. Apartheid in Crisis. New
    York: Vintage Books, 1986. 334 pp.

         The editor presents a collection of essays
    and interviews on the overall effect of apartheid
    in Africa.

24. Omitted.

Articles

25. Benenson, Robert. "South Africa's Total
    Strategy." Edit Res Rept (September 9,
    1983): 655-676.

    Benenson looks at the overall picture of
    South Africa regarding its posture on apartheid.

26. Burgess, M. Elaine. "Race and Social Change in
    South Africa: Divergent Perspectives." J
    Ethnic Stud 11: 1(1983): 47-71.

27. Crapanzano, Vincent. "Waiting (I)." NY 61 (March
    18, 1985): 50-52+.

    The author explores the social conditions,
    history and structure of the institution of
    apartheid in South Africa.

28. Glass, Humphrey. "Apartheidsgedagte: Apartheid
    Cultural Hegemony." Washington University,
    DAI, 1980, 41: 5262-A.

    Glass traces the social and political theory
    of apartheid and how whites justify the use of
    this system as an instrument for their existence
    in South Africa.

29. Gordenker, Leon. "Afrikaner Nationalism and the
    Plight of South Africa." Yale R 68 (June
    1979): 481-499.

    The author contends that "the sheer weight
    of growing internal opposition suggests that
    orthodox Afrikanerdom and its entailed racial
    policies must end in fragments, perhaps not at
    once but not after an eternity."

30. James, Wilmot G. "From Segregation to Apartheid:
         Miners and Peasants in the Making of a Racial
         Order, South Africa 1930-52." The University
         of Wisconsin-Madison, DAI 1982, 43: 3719-A.

         James states that "The motivational interest
     behind segregation and apartheid were to generate
     and regenerate a low wage black labor force and to
     systematically prevent black access to
     institutional forms of resistance to racial
     domination."

31. Kunnert, Dirk. "'Windows of Perils': Africa, the
         World and the 1980's." South Africa Intl 11,
         No. 1 (July, 1980): 1-20.

32. Lelyveld, Joseph. "South Africa Dream and
         Reality." NY Times M (September 22, 1985):
         40-43+.

         Lelyveld reveals some of the ideologies of
     whites in South Africa concerning apartheid.

33. Phillips, Lindsey. "South Africa's Future: No
         Easy Walk to Freedom." Work Papers for a New
         Soc (March/April 79): 25-43.

34. Pieres, J.B. "Nxele, Ntsikana and the Origins of
         the Xhasa Religious Reaction." Africa Hist
         20(1979): 51-61.

35. Temko, Ned. "Afrikaners: The Trek Continues."
         Chris Sci Mon (June 11, 1986): 18-19.

         Temko studies the historical development of
     the group of people responsible for instituting
     apartheid and the schism that's beginning to
     appear in their basic doctrine.

36. Theodoropoulous, Christor. "The Decolonization
         Approach to the Eradication of Apartheid."
         NY Univ Intl Law Pol 18 (Spring 1986): 899-
         920.

        The author contends that there are those who
don't understand the political and historical
development of apartheid.

37. Totten, Sam, ed. "Annotated Bibliography on
        Apartheid." <u>Soc Sci Rec</u>, 22:2 (Fall 1985):
        26-33.

38. Tutu, Desmond. "Dismantling Apartheid." <u>Soc Educ</u>
        49 (September 1985): 453-456.

        Tutu presents his views and ideals on
apartheid to the U.S. House Committee on Foreign
Affairs.

39. Ume, Kalu E. "The Origin of Apartheid in South
        Africa." <u>J of African Stud</u> 8: 4(1981):
        176-181.

40. Venter, Denis. "Black Africa and the Apartheid
        Issue: A South African Response." <u>Intl
        Contem African Stud</u> 1:1 (October 1981): 81-
        103.

41. Waas, Murray. "Destructive Engagement:
        Apartheid's Target U.S. Campaign." <u>Natl Rep</u>
        9 (Winter 1986): 12-27.

        Waas studies the policy of apartheid.

2.

ECONOMIC AND LABOR CONDITIONS

Monographs

42. African Worker Under Apartheid. Brussels:
International Confederation of Free Trade
Unions, May 1984.

43. Anti-Apartheid Movement: The Companies List: A
Directory of Companies Based in the UK That
Have Subsidiaries Operating in South Africa
and Namibia. London: Anti-Apartheid
Movement, 1982.

44. Automating Apartheid: U.S. Computer Exports to
South Africa and the Arms Embargo.
Philadelphia: NARMIC/American Friends Service
Committee, 1982. 107 pp.

Feels that too much emphasis is being placed
on the Sullivan Principles instead of the
products and services that are available from U.S.
companies to the white-controlled government.

45. Bailey, Martin. Oil Sanctions: South Africa's
Weak Link. New York: Centre Against
Apartheid, United Nations, 1980.

46. Boyer, Sandy. Black Unions in South Africa. New
York: The Africa Fund, 1982. 8 pp.

47. Cook, Allen. Akin to Slavery: Prison Labor in
         South Africa. London: International Defense
         and Aid Fund, 1982. 81 pp.

     Cook's main purpose in this work is to
     demonstrate the relationship of the prison labour
     system to other aspects of the system of
     apartheid.

48. Cooper, Carole. The African Woman's Handbook on
         the Law. Johannesburg: South Africa
         Institute of Race Relations, 1982. 41 pp.

49. _____. Strikes in South Africa. Johannesburg:
         South African Institute of Race Relations,
         1979.

50. Domini, Amy. Ethical Investing. Reading, Mass.:
         Addison - Wesley, 1984.

     In appendix D, the author gives the Sullivan
     Principles ratings for firms doing business in
     South Africa.

51. Eighth Report on the Signatory Companies to the
         Sullivan Principles. Philadelphia:
         International Council for Equality of
         Opportunity Principles, 1984. 44 pp.

52. First, Ruth, and Davies, Robert H. Migrant
         Labour to South Africa: A Sanctions
         Programme? Geneva: International University
         Exchange Fund, 1980. 35 pp.

53. Harsch, Ernest. South Africa: White Rule Black
         Revolt. New York: Pathfinder Press, 1980.
         352 pp.

     On pages 80-93, Harsch claims that "It was
     precisely to keep a firm rein on this powerful
     black working class and to prevent it from

translating its social weight into political power
that the white rulers erected the most elaborate
and extensive system of labor control in the
world."

54. Hauck, David. <u>Can Pretoria Be Saved? The</u>
    <u>Emergence of Business Activism in South</u>
    <u>Africa.</u> Washington, D.C.: Investor
    Responsibility Research Center, 1986. 56 pp.

    Hauck states that "Business men are also
    concerned that unless they distinguish themselves
    from the government, blacks will equate the
    capitalist economic system with the racist
    apartheid system-an attitude they fear could lead
    to disastrous consequences for them if and when a
    black government comes to power."

55. _____. <u>U.S. Corporate Withdrawal from South</u>
    <u>Africa: The Likely Impact on Political</u>
    <u>Change.</u> Washington, D.C.: Investor
    Responsibility Research Center, 1986. 22 pp.

56. International Labour Office. <u>Special Report of</u>
    <u>the Director-General on the Application of</u>
    <u>the Declaration Concerning the Policy of</u>
    <u>Apartheid in South Africa.</u> Geneva: The
    Office, 1986. 186 pp.

57. <u>Investment in Apartheid: A List of Companies With</u>
    <u>Investment and Interest in South Africa.</u>
    Brussels: International Confederation of
    Free Trade Unions, 1981. 40 pp.

    This is an updated list which names 3035
    companies doing business or having investments in
    South Africa.

58. Levy, Norman. <u>Discriminatory Labour Legislation</u>
    <u>and Practices in South Africa in the Field</u>
    <u>and Farm Labour.</u> Geneva: International
    Labour Office, 1985. 55 pp.

59. Macshane, Denis. Power! Black Workers, Their
     Unions and the Struggle for Freedom in South
     Africa. Boston: South End Press, 1984. 195
     pp.

60. Murray, Martin J. South African Capitalism and
     Black Political Opposition. Cambridge,
     Massachusetts: Schenkman, 1982. 773 pp.

     Murray attempts to provide a broad historical
     overview of the socioeconomic developments and
     changes that have taken place over the past three
     hundred years. Also, he seeks to explain the
     relationship between capitalist developments in
     that country and various forms of racial
     discrimination practiced there.

61. Myers, Desaix, III. Business and Labor in South
     Africa. Washington: Investor Responsibility
     Research Center, May 1987.

62. _____. U.S. Business in South Africa: The
     Economic, Political and Moral Issues.
     Bloomington: Indiana University Press, 1980.

63. Omitted.

64. Sampson, Anthony. Black and Gold: Tycoons,
     Revolutionaries, and Apartheid. New York:
     Pantheon Books, 1987.

     Sampson observes the practices and policies
     of multinationals and important South African
     firms that lend support to and benefit from the
     system of apartheid.

65. Schmidt, Elizabeth. Decoding Corporate
     Camouflage: U.S. Business Support for
     Apartheid. Washington: Institute for Policy
     Studies, 1980. 127 pp.

     Schmidt criticizes the Sullivan Principles as
     a smoke screen to protect U.S. companies doing
     business in South Africa.

66. Speaking Out: Secret Interviews With Black
    Workers in South Africa. London: Christian
    Concern for Southern Africa, 1982. 82 pp.

67. Stadler, Alfred. South Africa: The Political
    Economy of Apartheid. New York: St.
    Martin's Press, 1987.

Articles

68. Baigrie, James. "South African Trust Director
    Opposes Sanctions as Policy to Speed Reform."
    Trust & Es 124 (October 1985): 18-24.

69. "Barlow Rand: Seeking a Stable Labor Force
    Despite Apartheid." Bus Week (February 9,
    1981): 90+.

    Examines the strategy of one of South
    Africa's largest companies to meet its skilled
    workers' needs.

70. Battersby, John D. "Sanctions: The South African
    Government, with Private Sector Complicity,
    Has Already Devised Methods for Circumventing
    the Array of Economic Sanctions Imposed by
    Its Major Western Trading Partners." Africa
    Rep 32 (January/February 1987): 4-10.

71. Belknap, Timothy. "Laboring Under Apartheid."
    Africa Rep 30 (May-June 1985): 57+.

    The author contends that economics rather
    than politics will prove to be the key for
    bringing about a structural change in the
    institution of apartheid.

72. Blumenthal, J.P. "The South African Economy:
    Potential and Pitfalls." Wld Today
    36:9(September 1980): 334-342.

    Blumenthal contends that economic factors do
    contribute to socio-political change and seeks to
    explain how these conditions apply to the
    situation in South Africa.

73. _____. "South Africa: Economic Responses to
       International Pressures." Wld Today 41
       (December 1985): 218-221.

       Blumenthal examines the impact of the
sanctions placed upon South Africa and how they
might effect the economy.

74. Carson, James, and Fleshman, Michael. "Dollars
       for Apartheid: A State Department Cable
       Recalculates U.S. Investments in South Africa
       at Five Times the Previous Count." Multinatl
       4(November 1983): 18-21.

75. Chettle, John H. "The Law and Policy of
       Divestment of South African Stock." Law and
       Pol Int Bus 15(1983): 445-528.

       Chettle examines the portfolios of South
African companies and other institutions that
profit from the racial policies of that country.

76. Cock, Jacklyn. "Disposable Nannies: Domestic
       Servants in the Political Economy of South
       Africa." R African Pol Econ (May 1981):63-
       83.

77. Coker, Christopher. "Collective Bargaining as an
       Internal Sanction: The Role of U.S.
       Corporations in South Africa." Jnl Mod Afric
       Stud 19 (1981): 647-665.

       Coker states that "Many multinational
corporations now recognize that collective
bargaining is much more likely to lead to

improvements in working conditions and to
reductions in wage disparities between white and
non-white labour than any initiatives on their
part."

78. Cooper, John Howard. "Economic Sanctions and the
South African Economy." Intl Affairs Bull
7:2 (1983): 25-47.

79. Davies, Robert. "Capital Restructuring and the
Modification of the Racial Division of Labour
in South Africa." J Afri Con Stud 5 (April
1979): 181-98.

80. De Clercq, Francine. "Apartheid and the Organized
Labour Movement." R African Pol Econ (April
1979) 69-77.

81. Denison, Ray. "The Economics of Apartheid." AFL-
CIO Free Trade Union News 35 (June 1980): 5-
8.

Denison talks about the role of U.S.
companies in South Africa regarding investment and
trade.

82. "The Forum: TNC'S and South Africa." CTC Reporter
(Spring 1985): 34-37.

Examines the status and position of the major
corporations with regard to the racial policy of
that country.

83. Gaitskell, Deborah. "Class, Race and Gender:
Domestic Workers in South Africa." R African
Pol Econ (Fall 1984): 86-108.

Gaitskell examines the historical and present
day status of domestic service and what role it
plays in South Africa's political and economic
system.

84. Gould, William B. "Black Unions in South Africa:
    Labor Law Reform and Apartheid." Stanford J
    Intl Law 17 (Winter 1981): 99-162.

85. Grant, Charles. "The Banks Abandon South Africa."
    Euromony (December 1985): 64-65, 67-68, 71,
    73, 75, 77, 79-80.

    Grant examines the effect on South Africa's
    economy due to American bank cutoffs of credit.

86. Greenberg, Stanley. "Economic Growth and
    Political Change: The South Africa Case." J
    Mod Afric Stud (1981): 667-704.

    Greenberg studies the effect that the economy
    can play in altering the political policies in
    South Africa and how politics can impede the
    growth of that country's economy.

87. Harrop, Mark D. "The Fast-Ticking Time Bomb in
    South African Mines: National Union of Mine
    Workers: South Africa's Great Black Hope."
    Bus & Soc R (Spring 1984): 52-55.

    The author contends that black workers in
    general are becoming a force in South Africa's
    mining sector that will have to be dealt with on a
    less discriminatory basis by the government and
    management.

88. Harsch, Ernest. "South Africa: Apartheid's Great
    Land Theft; How Racist System Keeps Blacks
    from Farming; A Revolution for Black Land
    Rights." Inter Pr 23 (December 30, 1985):
    782-788.

89. Haworth, Nigel. "Sanctions Against South Africa:
    Do Black Workers Want Them?" Internat Labour
    Rpts (January/February 1986): 23-25.

Haworth examines the growing debate in South Africa on the topic of disinvestment.

90. Holland, Martin. "The European Community and South Africa: Economic Reality or Political Rhetoric?" Pol Stud 33 (Summer 1985): 399-417.

Holland describes and analyzes the Code of Conduct for European firms operating in South Africa.

91. "How Multi-National Corporations Impede South African Revolution." Afr Communist No. 76 (1979): 69-80.

92. Omitted.

93. Lelyveld, Joseph. "Oppenheimer of South Africa." NY Times M 8 (1983): 32-35+

The author looks at the diamond king and what he is trying to do to bring about economic reform in South Africa.

94. Lewin, Peter. "The Prohibitive Cost of Apartheid." Intercollegiate R 21 (Winter 1985/1986): 25-31.

95. Lipton, Merle. "The Debate About South Africa: Neo-Marxists and Neo-Liberals." Afric Affairs 78: 310 (January 1979): 57-80.

Lipton examines incomes, job advancement, and unemployment of Africans under the present system of apartheid. Also, the author discusses the policy of constructive engagement as a viable means of changing the system in South Africa.

96. "The MNC [multinational corporation] Record in
     South Africa Employment." Multi Bus no. 2
     (1985): 33-35.

          Gives a breakdown of the U.S. and European
     companies' employment of blacks in their
     corporations.

97. Marsh, Pearl-Alice. "Labor Reform and Security
     Repression in South Africa: Botha's Strategy
     for Stabilizing Racial Domination in the
     1980s." Issue 12:3-4 (Fall-Winter 1982):
     49-55.

          Marsh analyzes the growth of the African
     trade unions and the government's attempt to
     control their growth and power.

98. Mason, David. "Industrialization, Race and Class
     Conflict in South Africa: Towards a
     Sociological Resolution of a Reopened
     Debate." Ethnic & Racial Stud 3(April 1980):
     140-155.

99. Omitted.

100. Porter, Richard C. "International Trade and
     Investment Sanctions: Potential Impact on
     the South African Economy." J Can Res 23:
     No. 4 (December 1979): 579-612.

          Porter states that, "The purpose of this
     paper is to clarify the theory of international
     economic sanctions and to provide estimates of the
     short-run economic impact on South Africa of
     externally imposed reductions of the imports and
     capital flows into that country."

101. Quinlan, Martin. "South Africa: Oil Embargo
     Would Be Impractical." Pet Econ 52 (November
     1986): 401-403.

102. Relly, Gavin. "The Costs of Disinvestment."
     Foreign Pol 63 (Summer 1986): 131-146.

     Relly explores the relationship between the
     business sector and the government in South Africa
     and what is being done by the business leaders in
     that country to bring an end to apartheid.

103. Schomer, Howard. "South Africa: Beyond Fair
     Employment; Action That Companies Can Take
     Now to Foster Justice and Stability." Harv
     Bus R 61 (May/June 1983): 145-156.

104. Seidman, Ann. "Why U.S. Corporations Should Get
     Out of South Africa." Issue 9:1,2 (1979):
     37-41.

     Seidman discusses the status of U.S.
     corporations in South Africa and what should be
     done to keep a closer look at their activities.

105. Sherman, Stratford P. "Scoring Corporate Conduct
     in South Africa." Fortune 110 (July 9,
     1984): 168-172.

     Sherman examines the Sullivan Principles and
     how U.S. companies adhere to these rules and
     regulations.

106. Slatter, Robert Bruce. "Companies That Hide
       Behind the Sullivan Principles; Some
       Nonsigners Behave Better Than Some Sullivan
       Signatories." Bus & Soc R (Spring 1984):
       15-18.

       Slatter studies the employment practices of
     U.S. corporations with affiliates operating in
     South Africa.

107. "Slipping Through the Cracks: The Status of Black
       Women." R Black Pol Econ 14 (Fall-Winter
       1985-1986): 300 pp.

       This special issue examines the role of black
     women in the labor force and the job training
     programs set aside for them.

108. Somerville, Keith. "South Africa: Business
       Sense, Worried About the Economic Effects of
       Political Instability, South Africa's White
       Businessmen Have Voiced Their Concern Both to
       the Government and the ANC." Africa (October
       1985): 30-33.

109. "South African Crisis: Shame of UK Stake in
       Apartheid." Labour Res 74 (Summer 1985):
       227-229.

       This article contains a list of British
     companies and the number of their employees that
     are still operating in South Africa.

110. "South Africa's Foot-Dragging Vexes U.S.
       Companies." Bus Week (October 20 1980): 56-
       58.

       U.S. companies are hesitant about increasing
     their exposure in South Africa, due to the critics
     abroad and the militant black workers in South
     Africa.

111. Stultz, Newell M. "Black Consumers in South
     Africa: A Rising Power?" <u>Akron Business and
     Economic Rev</u> 12 (Spring 1981): 11 pp.

112. "TNC's and South Africa." <u>CTC Reporter</u> (Spring
     1985): 28-33.

     Covers such things as the codes of conduct
regarding employment practices of transnational
corporations operating in South Africa and
examines the text of the Sullivan Principles.

113. Urdang, Stephanie. "Removals: Destroying
     Communities to Cheapen Labor; How Apartheid
     Depends on Despair." <u>Chr and Crisis</u> 45
     (February 4/18/1985): 14-19.

     The author believes that the removal of
blacks is strongly connected to the economic
system of that country. Mainly, it is a vehicle
for establishing a supply of cheap labor.

114. Vose, W.J. "Wiehahn and Riekert Revisited: A
     Review of Prevailing Black Labour Conditions
     in South Africa." <u>Inter Labour R</u> 124 (July-
     August 1985): 447-464.

     This article concludes that the plight of
blacks in the labor force has not improved even
after the establishment of a new constitution.

115. Walt, Vivienne. "The Economy Pressure Point."
     <u>Africa Rep</u> 31 (March-April 1986): 60-63.

     Looks at South Africa's attempt to negotiate
with foreign banks for loans because of criticism
by consumer boycotts and international financiers.

116. Watson, Russell. "Time Has Run Out." <u>Newsweek</u>
     106 (September 9, 1985): 28-32.

     The author states that "South Africa's rulers
win every street battle but seem to be losing the
war as financial confidence crumbles."

117. Wellings, Paul. "Industrial Decentralization
        Under Apartheid: The Relocation of Industry
        to the South African Periphery." Wld Dev 14
        (January 1986): 1-38.

118. Wicker, Tom. "Should American Business Pull Out
        of South Africa?" NY Times M (June 3, 1979):
        31, 33, 36-37, 72, 74, 76, 78.

        Wicker talks about the positive and negative
    aspects of U.S. companies divesting in South
    Africa.

119. Wiseman, Mark. "Recent South African Labor
        Legislation: Assessing the New Rights of
        Black Workers." Boston Col Internat and Comp
        Law R 9 (Winter 1986): 163-197.

        Wiseman discusses the history of black labor
    and the conditions in South Africa as a result of
    recent legislative changes affecting black labor.

120. Zille, H. "Survey of Black Worker in South Finds
        That Most Oppose Cuts in Foreign
        Investments." Chron Higher Educ 29 (November
        21, 1984): 29-30.

        Black organizations question the reliability
    of this study because it was partly funded by the
    U.S., which supports the policy of constructive
    engagement.

                              Documents

121. Maxey, Phyllis. American Business in South Africa.
        Instructor's Guide and Student Material.
        Washington, D.C.: Educational Resources
        Information Center. 1982. 44pp. (ED 238811).

122. U.N. General Assembly. A/Conf. 94/BP/16. The
     Effects of Apartheid on the Employment of
     Women in South Africa and a History of the
     Role of Women in the Trade Unions. 11 June
     1980. 44pp.

123. U.N. General Assembly. E/C. 10/AC. 4/1985/2.
     Examination of the Activities of
     Transnational Corporations in South Africa
     and Namibia. Measures Regarding the
     Activities of Transnational Corporations in
     South Africa and Namibia. Report of the
     Secretary-General 19 August 1985. 29pp.

124. U.S. Congress. House. Economic Sanctions and
     their Potential Impact on U.S. Corporate
     Involvement in South Africa. 99th Cong., 1st
     Sess., January 31, 1985. Washington, D.C.
     Congressional Information Service, 105pp.
     (H381-51).

3.

POLITICS AND GOVERNMENT

Monographs

125. Adams, Heribert. *Ethnic Power Mobilized: Can South Africa Change?* New Haven: Yale University Press, 1979. 308 pp.

     The author seeks to determine if South Africa can change its political doctrine without destroying itself in the process.

126. _____. *South Africa Without Apartheid: Dismantling Racial Domination.* Berkeley: University of California Press, 1986. 315 pp.

     The author discusses the government in South Africa and the current outlook for change in that country's system of racial indifference.

127. Austin, Dennis. *South Africa 1984.* London: Routledge, Chapman & Hall, Inc., 1984. 80 pp.

     Austin says, "The question examined in this essay is whether South Africa can fill the gap left by the withdrawal of colonial power from Southern Africa or whether it will itself become a battlefield. It is the central problem in the familiar puzzle about National Party rule whether it can truly change in order to survive."

128. Breytenbach, Willie. *The Botha Strategy and The Eighties.* Johannesburg: South Africa Foundation, July 1980.

129. Carter, Gwendolyn M. Which Way Is South Africa
     Going? Bloomington: Indiana University
     Press, 1980. 162 pp.

     In Chapter 2, Carter observes the rise of
     Afrikaner nationalism and how it has shaped the
     current policy of separate development in South
     Africa.

130. Cooper, Carole. Survey of Race Relations in South
     Africa, 1983. Johannesburg: South African
     Institute of Race Relations, 1984.   700 pp.

     On pages 7-28, the author gives an overview
     of the various white political parties in South
     Africa and their feelings about race relations in
     their country.

131. Fatton, Robert, Jr. "Class and Nationalism in
     South Africa." Ph.D. Diss. University of
     Notre Dame, 1981.

     Fatton examines the changes of black politics
     from 1952-1976.

132. Greenberg, Stanley B. Legitimating the
     Illegitimate: States, Markets, and
     Resistance in South Africa. Berkeley:
     University of California Press, 1987.   300
     pp.

133. Hachten, William A., and Giffard, C.A. The Press
     and Apartheid: Repression and Propaganda in
     South Africa. Madison: University Wisconsin
     Press, 1984. 336 pp.

134. Hanf, T. South Africa: The Prospects of Peaceful
     Change-An Empirical Inquiry Into the
     Possibility of Democratic Conflict
     Negotiation. Bloomington: Indiana Univ.
     Pr., 1981.

135. Harrison, D. The White Tribe of Africa: South
     Africa in Perspective. Los Angeles:
     University of California Press, 1981. 307 pp.

The author traces the social, legal, and
political developments of the Afrikaners through
the mid-80's.

136. Horrell, Muriel. Race Relations as Regulated by
     Law in South Africa, 1948-1979.
     Johannesburg: South African Institute of
     Race Relations, 1982.

137. Lapping, Brian. Apartheid: A History. New York:
     G. Braziller, 1986.

     Lapping details the National Party's
     philosophy of apartheid and how they used this
     ideology to gain and remain in power.

138. Leach, Graham. South Africa: No Easy Path to
     Peace. Boston: Routledge, Chapman & Hall,
     Inc., 1986. 266 pp.

     The author attempts to provide an account of
     that country's political situation and the ongoing
     debate in the U.S. regarding divestment and U.S.
     relations with South Africa.

139. Leatt, James, ed. Contending Ideologies in South
     Africa. Grand Rapids: W.B. Eerdmans, 1986.
     318 pp.

140. Lemon, Anthony. White Voters and Political Change
     in South Africa, 1981-1983. Oxford: School
     of Geography, University of Oxford, 1984. 40
     pp.

     In this paper, Lemon examines the
     developments of a new constitution that would give
     coloreds and Indians the right to vote.

141. Libby, Ronald T. Toward an Africanized U.S.
     Policy for Southern Africa: A Strategy for
     Increasing Political Leverage. Berkeley:
     University of California Press, 1980. 119
     pp.

In Chapter 1, Libby states that "Ultimately
it is the confidence of the Afrikaners in the NP
and in the Nation that they can survive and
prosper through military domination that will
determine the extent and speed with which
structural changes in the South African regime and
in the region will occur."

142. Lodge, Tom. Black Politics in South Africa Since
     1945. White Plains: Longman Inc., 1983. 389
     pp.

143. Magubane, Bernard Makhosezive. The Political
     Economy of Race and Class in South Africa.
     New York: Monthly Review Press, 1979. 364
     pp.

     Magubane covers the sociological and
     historical approach of oppression and racial
     unequality in South Africa.

144. Malberbe, Paul N. A Scenario for Peaceful Change
     in South Africa. Cape Town: College
     Tutorial Press, 1986. 61 pp.

145. Marks, Shula, ed. The Politics of Race, Class,
     and Nationalism in Twentieth-Century South
     Africa. White Plains: Longman Inc., 1987.

146. Mermelstein, David, ed. South Africa, the
     Struggle Against White Racist Rule. New
     York: Grove Press, 1986.

147. The National Party: And What About the Black
     People? Federal Information Service of the
     National Party, April 1985.

148. Neuhaus, Richard J. Dispensations: The Future of
     South Africa as South Africans See It. Grand
     Rapids: William Eerdmans Publ., 1986. 317
     pp.

     The author covers views from Tutu, the Zulus
     and their Chief, Indian professionals and
     businessmen, Afrikaners, and the English community

on the subjects of race, justice, and the notion
of peaceful change.

149. Parker, Frank J. <u>South Africa: Lost
Opportunities</u>. Lexington: Lexington Books,
1983. 290 pp.

The author talks about politics and its
relationship to race in South Africa from 1977-
1982.

150. Price, Robert M., ed. <u>The Apartheid Regime:
Political Power and Racial Domination</u>.
Berkeley: Institute of International
Studies, University of California, 1980. 376
pp.

Examines the inner workings of the Afrikaners
and their control over the government.

151. <u>Repression in a Time of Reform</u>. Johannesburg:
United Democratic Front, November, 1984. 81
pp.

152. <u>South Africa: Inprisonment Under the Pass Laws</u>.
New York: Amnesty International, 1986. 105
pp.

Examines the use of the government's action
in enforcing apartheid through the identification
system.

153. Spiro, Peter. <u>Better Now Than Never: Economic
and Social Reforms in South Africa</u>.
Washington: Cato Institute, 1987. 23 pp.

Spiro feels that through methods of
deregulating the South African economy and giving
private property to blacks, it would help bring
about a smoother transition to a new form of
government.

154. Standbridge, Roland. "Contemporary African
Political Organizations and Movements."
Chapter IV in <u>The Apartheid Regime:</u>

Political Power and Racial Domination.
Berkeley: Institute of International
Studies, 1980.

The author focuses on the major black
movements and political organizations and their
fight to gain equality.

155. Thompson, L.M. "The Parting of the Ways in South
     Africa." The Transfer of Power in Africa.
     Edited by P. Gifford and W.R. Louis. New
     Haven: Yale Univ. Press, 1982, pp. 417-444.

The author attempts to explain the political
process in South Africa and how it developed into
the racial system that it is today.

156. _____. The Political Mythology of Apartheid. New
     Haven: Yale University Press, 1985. 293 pp.

Thompson seeks to explain the economic,
historical, demographic, and international
relations of South Africa and how they relate to
the racial order of that country.

157. _____. South African Politics. New Haven: Yale
     University Press, 1982.

The author sets out to describe the political
power of South Africa and how it actually
operates. Also, he seeks to explain the
demographic, economic, and historical conditions
as they relate to the racial order of that
country.

158. Omitted.

159. Van der Berghe, P.L. The Liberal Dilemma in South
     Africa. London: Croom Helm, 1979.

Examines how it is possible to create a nonracial democracy in South Africa without the use
of violence between blacks and whites.

160. Van Zyl Slabbert, F. <u>South Africa's Options:</u>
     <u>Strategies for Sharing Power</u>. New York: St.
     Martin's Press, 1979. 193 pp.

     The author attempts to present a political
     analysis of the government of South Africa and
     alternatives to what can be done to bring this
     government to the negotiating table with the
     blacks of that country.

161. Welsh, David. <u>South Africa's Options: Strategies</u>
     <u>for Sharing Power</u>. New York: St. Martin's
     Press, 1979. 196 pp.

                        Articles

162. Adams, Heribert. "Reforms in South Africa: More
     Rhetoric than Substance." <u>Intl Perspect</u>
     (January/February 1981): 24-26.

163. _____. "The Ultraright in South Africa and Ethnic
     Nationalism." <u>Can R Stud Natl</u> 14 (Spring
     1987): 83-92.

     Adams examines the various political and
     philosophical breaks within the Afrikaner
     Nationalist Coalition.

164. "Apartheid in South Africa: Setting the Stage for
     Change Without Innovation." <u>Guardian</u>
     (November 23, 1980):12.

165. "As South Africa's Whites Keep Iron Grip on
     Power." <u>U.S. News World Rep</u> 98 (May 13,
     1985): 40-41,44.

     This article looks at the constant demands by
     blacks in South Africa trying to share in the
     political structure of that country.

166. Barber, James. "South Africa: A Society at War
     with Itself." Wld Today 41 (July 1985): 129-
     132.

          Barber examines the politics and political
     parties in that country. Also, he mentions the
     government policies and the attitudes of the
     people concerning the politics and parties.

167. _____. "Afrikanerdom in Disarray." Wld Today 38
     (July/August 1982): 288-296.

          The author talks about the formation of the
     National Conservative Party due to disputes in the
     main party over the system of apartheid.

168. Boesak, Allan. "Is Reconciliation Possible in
     South Africa?" Chr Cent 101 (May 23, 1984):
     546-550.

          In this interview, Boesak discusses his views
     of the dangers and causes of the violence that is
     taking place in South Africa and measures that can
     be implemented in order to bring about reform.

169. _____. "Tensions Are Deepening, Anger Rising."
     Chr and Crisis 44 (November 26, 1984): 444-
     447.

          Boesak contends that blacks in South Africa
     are becoming impatient because of the government's
     racist policies.

170. Omitted.

171. Bradlee, Ben, Jr. "If We Stick to Our Guns, It Is
     Not a Streak of Meanness. It's Our Very
     History." Boston Globe Mag (December 29,
     1985): 13-16, 20-22, 26-28.

Bradlee contends that the South African
government will make changes in its policies when
they feel the time is right, regardless of what
the blacks or the rest of the world might want.

172. Breytenbach, Breyten. "The South African
     Wasteland." New Repub 193 (November 4,
     1985): 32-38.

     Contends that the political system of South
Africa is not as democratic as they pretend it to
be, but quite similar to that of a communist type
regime.

173. Butcher, Goler T. "The Resolution of the American
     Bar Association, Against Apartheid." Howard
     Law J 28 (1985): 649-675.

     Examines statements made by this association
opposing apartheid, including the limitations set
against the black majority.

174. Buthelezi, Mangosuthu G. "Interview: Mangosuthu
     G. Buthelezi." J Def Dipl 4 (August 1986):
     12-15.

     This article focuses on Buthelezi's feelings
concerning the African National Congress and other
political and governmental issues.

175. _____. "The Politics of Negotiations in South
     Africa: The Real Problems." Round Table
     (July 1987): 294-301.

176. _____. "South Africa: A Testimony." Two Thirds
     6:2 (1985): 11-29.

     Buthelezi discusses the status of the
struggle for equal opportunity for blacks in all
walks of life in South Africa.

177. "Can South Africa Avoid Race War?" US News World
     Rep 99 (August 26, 1985): 20-24.

This article focuses on the increase of
violence among blacks and whites in South Africa
and the U.S. involvement in bringing this
situation to a peaceful settlement.

178. "Can South Africa Save Itself?" Newsweek 106
     (August 19, 1985): 14-20+.

     This article alludes to Botha's call for
reforms as a way of bringing an end to the system
of apartheid.

179. Christenson, Ronald. "The Civil Religion of
     Apartheid: Afrikanerdom's Covenant."
     Midwest Q 22 (Winter, 1979): 137-146.

     Christenson talks about the National Party
and the reasons why they adhere to the doctrine of
apartheid.

180. Cowell, Alan. "The Struggle: Power and Politics
     in South Africa's Black Trade Unions." N Y
     Times M (June 15, 1986): 14-27.

181. Daniel, A. "South Africa Targets the Churches."
     Chr & Crisis 43 (July 11, 1983): 285-289.

     Daniel talks about the judicial commission
that was formed by the government to inquire into
the affairs of the South African Council of
Churches and their involvement with groups trying
to bring an end to apartheid.

182. Dash, Samuel. "A Rare Talk with Nelson Mandela."
     NY Times M (July 7, 1985): 20-22.

     In this interview, Mandela outlines the way
he would like to see South Africa governed after
apartheid is dismantled.

183. De St. Jorre, John. "South Africa Embattled."
     For Affairs 65, no. 3(1987):538-563.

Studies the events and reforms instituted by Botha in 1986. Also, the author examines the United States policy of constructive engagement.

184. Denemark, Robert A. "The Political Economy of Repression and Reform in South Africa." Afr Today 29 (Third Quarter 1982): 5-31.

185. "Donald B. Sole; South African Ambassador to the United States." Africa Rep 26 (September/October 1981): 14-19.

In this interview, Sole talks about the country's racial policies and political conditions.

186. Fine, Daniel I. "Pretoria's Turn Toward More Liberal Racial Policies." Bus Week (April 23, 1979): 65.

Fine discusses the recent proposed changes in the race laws regarding statutory job discrimination and granting legal recognition to black trade unions.

187. Fourie, Bernardus. "Spotlight on South Africa." Common Cause Mag 11 (May-June 1985): 28-32.

In an extensive interview, South Africa's Ambassador explains his country's policy of apartheid and how it is good for the entire country.

188. Frankel, Philip. "The Politics of Poverty: Political Competition in Soweto." Can J Afr Stud 14 (No. 2, 1980): 201-20.

189. _____. "Soweto: Urban Politics, Poverty and Race in Apartheid Society." Ph.D. Princeton University, DAI, 1982, 43: 2436-A.

Factors concerning political resources and how they affect race and poverty in urban areas are examined by this author.

190. "Gathering Hints of Change." Time 126 (August 19, 1985): 22-26.

   This article examines the increase of violence that has taken place in South Africa and looks at Botha's attempts to make some type of concessions that might affect the structure of apartheid.

191. Giliomee, Hermann. "Constructing Afrikaner Nationalism." J Asian African Stud 18 (1983): 83-98.

   The author states that "The Afrikaner Nationalist Movement had its roots not only in the Africaners' economic condition but also in their status needs, which demanded political autonomy and due recognition of their language."

192. Grotpeter, John. "Changing South Africa." Curr Hist 78 (March, 1980): 119-23, 134-36.

   The author discusses some of the legal jargon and movements of the South African government as a means of taking some criticism off that country's system of apartheid.

193. Grundy, Kenneth W. "South Africa's Domestic Strategy." Curr Hist (March 1983): 110-114+.

   Grundy describes the constitutional reform in South Africa and how it has brought about changes in political and economic freedoms of blacks and whites.

194. Hale, Frederick. "South Africa: Defending the Laager." Curr Hist 84 (April 1985): 155-158, 194-186.

   The author states that it is unlikely that the South African government will soften its policy of apartheid due to sanctions and economic recession.

195. Horowitz, Donald L. "After Apartheid." <u>New Repub</u>
     193 (November 4, 1985): 19-23.

     Horowitz examines the problems that will
exist for blacks when apartheid is abolished and
what institutions will replace it.

196. Huntington, Samuel P. "Reform and Stability in
     South Africa." <u>Int Sec</u> 6(Spring 1982): 3-25.

197. Johnson, Paul. "The Race for South Africa." <u>Comt</u>
     80(Summer, 1985): 27-32.

     The author states that the ANC appears to be
destroying the moderate elements within the
coloured, Asian and black populations in their
effort to bring an end to apartheid.

198. Karis, Thomas G. "South African Liberation: The
     Communist Factor." <u>For Affairs</u> 65 (Winter
     1986-87): 267-287.

     Karis contends that by concentrating on the
communist elements, the U.S. could be
misinterpreting the true meaning of the ANC.

199. Knight, Robin. "South Africa Teeters on a Knife-
     Edge." <u>US News World Rep</u> 99 (September 2,
     1985): 27-31.

     Knight looks at the political situation in
South Africa and what steps are being used to
bring about a peaceful change in that country.
Also, the author examines the various political
parties among blacks and whites in South Africa.

200. _____. "South African Voting Puts U.S. on the
     Spot." <u>US News World Rep</u> 90 (May 11, 1981):
     65-66.

     Reagan's policy is running into trouble due
to Botha's reluctance to reform that country's
policy of apartheid and grant independence to
Namibia.

201. Legassick, Martin. "South Africa in Crisis: What
     Route to Democracy?" _Afric Affairs_ 84
     (October 1985): 587-603.

     Examines the constant struggle for the
     institution of democracy as a replacement for the
     system of apartheid.

202. Magubane, Bernard. "The Mounting Class and
     National Struggles in South Africa." _Review_
     8 (1984): 197-231.

203. Ngeokavane, Cecil. "Religious and Moral
     Legitimations of Apartheid in Nederduitse,
     Gereformeerde Kerk, Nationalist Party and
     Broederbond, 1948-Present (South Africa)."
     Ph.D. Emory University, _DAI_, 1986, 47:4110-A.

     The author examines the reasons and
     justifications used by the NGK party to continue
     their oppression of blacks in South Africa. Also,
     she seeks to explain how religion has played a
     major part in perpetuating apartheid.

204. North, James. "Capitalism and Apartheid." _New
     Repub_ 181: 18 (May 5, 1979): 20-23.

     North notes the various political factions or
     groups in South Africa and their feelings about
     sanctions and the system of apartheid.

205. O'Brien, Conor C. "What Can Become of South
     Africa?" _Atl Mo_ 257 (March 1986): 41-50+.

     The author talks about the methods used by
     those opposed to the system of apartheid.

206. O'Meara, Patrick. "South Africa: No New
     Political Dispensation." _Curr Hist_ 83 (March
     1984): 105-108.

Examines the acceptance of a new constitution that allows coloureds and Indians to elect their own representatives to separate Parliaments.

207. "Organizing the Struggle: Cyril Ramaphosa, General Secretary, National Union of Mine Workers; As Leader of South Africa's Largest Union; Cyril Ramaphosa Has Played a Key Role in Forging Black Trade Union Unity and Broadening Its Involvement in the Wider Political Struggle." Africa Rep 3 (March/April 1986): 10-14.

Covers an interview about black organized labor in South Africa and their efforts to bring an end to apartheid.

208. Pascoe, William. "Indaba We Trust: South Africa's Last Best Hope for Racial Peace." Policy R (Winter 1987): 42-45.

Discusses the idea of a proposal to dismantle apartheid in two homelands and bring them together under one government.

209. Pogrund, Benjamin. "Falling Apartheid." New Repub 193 (September 9, 1985): 11-14.

The author feels that the Afrikaners' power has not been challenged to its full extent and that they will not give up their philosophy without a major fight.

210. Potts, Lee W. "Law as a Tool of Social Engineering: The Case of the Republic of South Africa." Boston Col Internat and Comp Law R 5 (Winter 1982): 1-50.

Potts examines the policies and laws aimed at the various racial groups in that country.

211. Rayapen, Lewis C.A. "South Africa: Constitutional Change or Violent Revolution?" Internat J World Peace 3 (April/June 1986): 37-65.

Rayapen comments on apartheid and the
position taken by the South African government,
the African National Congress, and other groups
opposing that government.

212. Reed, David. "South Africa: Will White Rule End?"
     Read Digest 128 (February 1986): 146-153.

Reed concludes that the forecast for South
Africa is that more discontent and disorder will
continue for blacks and the government will
continue to resist giving any type of political
power to blacks.

213. Ropp, Klaus, Baron. "Power Sharing Versus
     Partition in South Africa." Aust Out (August
     1981): 158-168.

214. Salpeter, Eliahu. "The Agony of Reform in South
     Africa: Modifying Apartheid." New Leader 63
     (July 28, 1980): 4-7.

Salpeter examines the 12-point program
announced by Botha that was designed to ease the
regulations regarding the policy of racial
segregation.

215. Saul, John S. "The Crisis in South Africa: Class
     Defense, Class Revolution." Mo R 33
     (July/August 1981): 1-156.

216. Schwartz, Joseph M. "Black Politics in South
     Africa." Dissent 33 (Winter 1986): 5-14.

Schwartz examines past events that have led
to the current situation in South Africa.

217. Serfontein, Hennie. "Stepping into Darkness: As
     the South African Government Tries to Cope
     with Mounting Political Opposition, a New
     Constitution Has Been Enshrined Which Offers
     Power-sharing to Asians and Coloureds, But
     Still Ignores the African Majority." Africa
     (August 1980): 42-44.

218. Omitted.

219. "South Africa." <u>Wld Press Rev</u> 32 (November 1985):
     35-40.

     Examines some of the political reforms that
     Botha instituted and how various groups within
     that country reacted to them.

220. "South Africa: Botha's Brazilian Option or the
     Third Phase of Apartheid." <u>Africa</u> (May 1980):
     62-64.

     Botha attempts to ease restrictions on the
     English-speaking business community, blacks and
     those of mixed race in return for their political
     support.

221. "South Africa Under Botha." <u>Foreign Pol</u> (Spring
     1980): 126-142.

     The author says, "The United States must push
     and pull. It must continue to kick hard at South
     Africa's shins, but less often and less hard if
     and when Botha talks serious politics with
     Buthelezi, Motlana, and other leaders."

222. "South Africa's Agony." <u>Wld Press Rev</u> (June
     1985): 37-42.

     Talks about the political future of South
     Africa and what will become of the blacks and
     whites of that country.

223. "South Africa's Democratic Opposition: An
     Interview with Chief Buthelezi." <u>Am
     Spectator</u> 16 (March 1983): 13-15.

224. Southall, Roger. "A Note on Inkatha Membership."
     Afric Affairs 85 (October 1986): 573-592.

     The author examines this political
     organization and its potential importance in
     shaping the political outcome in South Africa.

225. Spicer, Michael. "Change in South Africa? Mr.
     P.W. Botha's Strategy and Policies." Wld
     Today (January 1980): 32-40.

     Botha discusses his views on the policy of
     separate development or apartheid.

226. Steward, James B. "Contemporary Patterns of
     Black-White Political Economic Inequality in
     the United States and South Africa." R Black
     Pol Econ 9 (Summer 1979): 359-391.

227. Streek, Barry. "Apartheid Under Siege." Africa
     Rep 30 (January/February 1985): 54-48.

     Streek contends that due to the enormous
     amount of domestic unrest and the constant
     pressure from the white right wing, Botha's
     government has begun to use oppressive tactics to
     deal with the situation in that country.

228. Swan, George Steven. "The Republic of South
     Africa Undertakes Its New Constitution.
     Pretoria Proves Objectionable to John C.
     Calhoun Himself." Thurg Marsh Law R 10
     (Spring 1985): 365-384.

     The author explains that the changes in the
     new constitution do not give equal representation
     to the blacks in South Africa.

229. Uhlig, Mark A. "Inside the African National
     Congress." NY Times M (October 12, 1986): 20-21+.

This article reveals that the U.S. is finally taking a closer look at the A.N.C. and its tactics of fighting apartheid.

230. Uys, Stanley. "South Africa Under Mr. Botha; The Future of White Rule and the Pressures from Outside." Round Table no. 273 (January 1979): 58-64.

Botha will continue to impose the basics of apartheid because his party has given him that mandate.

230a. Van Zyl Slabbert, F. "Sham Reform and Conflict Regulation in a Divided Society." J Asian African Stud, 18: 1-2 (1983): 34-48.

Slabbert examines the government of South Africa and its call for reforms of its current constitution.

231. Vollenhoven, Sylvia. "South Africa at the Crossroads." Third World Q 8 (April 1986): 486-506.

This article addresses the problems that exist in South Africa due, in part, to the government's political reform program.

232. Welsh, David. "Constitutional Changes in South Africa." Afric Affairs 83 (April 1984): 147-162.

Welsh observes the changes regarding the position of non-white population groups in South Africa. Also, he talks about the various sections of the Constitutional act of 1983.

233. Whitaker, Mark. "Politics of the Laager." Newsweek 106 (August 12, 1985): 36-38.

Whitaker examines the reactions of blacks and whites in South Africa over the use of the state of emergency declared by Botha.

Documents

234. U.N. General Assembly. A/35/439. Policies of
     Apartheid of the Government of South Africa:
     Letter Dated 5 September 1980 by the Special
     Committee Against Apartheid 16 September
     1980. 5 pp.

235. _____. A/36/190. Policies of Apartheid of the
     Government of South Africa: Letter Dated 10
     April 1981 from the Chairman of the Special
     Committee Against Apartheid to the Secretary-
     General 15 April 1981. 5 pp.

236. _____. A/36/319. Policies of Apartheid of the
     Government of South Africa: Letter Dated 11
     June 1981 From the Chairman of the Special
     Committee Against Apartheid to the Secretary-
     General 15 June 1981. 20 pp.

237. _____. A/Res/40/64. Policies of Apartheid of the
     Government of South Africa: Resolutions. 27
     January 1986. 27 pp.

4.

SOCIAL CONDITIONS

Monographs

238. <u>Apartheid Poverty, and Malnutrition</u>. Rome: Food
     and Agriculture Organization, 1982.   101 pp.

     The organization contends that the system of
     apartheid is a major hinderance to the social and
     economic welfare of the blacks in South Africa.

239. Archer, Robert, and Bouillan, Antoine.   <u>The South</u>
     <u>African Game: Sport and Racism</u>.   London:
     Zed Press, 1982.   325 pp.

     The authors attempt to show that there is a
     nonracial sports movement within South Africa.
     Also, they contend that sports is not a good
     vehicle for providing change in that country.

240. Carter, Gwendolyn M.   <u>Which Way Is South Africa</u>
     <u>Going</u>?   Bloomington: Indiana University
     Press, 1980.   162 pp.

     On pages 29-48, Carter details the
     correlation between homelands or black states and
     the system of apartheid.

241. Children Under Apartheid: In Photographs and
        Text. London: International Defense and Aid
        Fund for Southern Africa, January 1980. 118
        pp.

     Examines the psychological and physical
effects on the children who live under the laws of
apartheid.

242. Cooper, Carole. Survey of Race Relations in South
        Africa, 1983. Johannesburg: South African
        Institute of Race Relations, 1984. 700 pp.

     On pages 220-226, the author examines the
various places such as beaches, hospitals, hotels,
and transportation that are off limits to blacks.

243. Foster, Don. Detention and Torture in South
        Africa: Psychological, Legal and Historical
        Studies. New York: St. Martin's Press,
        1987.

     Foster examines the theory that detainees
held in prison under apartheid laws are frequently
subjected to brutal beatings, even though the
government denies it.

244. Goodwin, June. Cry Amandla! South African Women
        and the Question of Power. New York:
        Africana Publishing Co., 1984. 253 pp.

     Goodwin talks about the plight of black women
as domestic servants; included are personal
interviews with women who are domestic workers.

245. International Labour Office. International Labour
        Conference: 73rd Session 1987: Special
        Report of the Director-General on the
        Application of the Declaration Concerning the
        Policy of Apartheid in South Africa. Geneva:
        The Office, 1987. 180 pp.

     Studies the impact of apartheid on social and
economic conditions in South Africa.

246. James, Deborah. The Road From Doornkop: A Case
     Study of Removals and Resistance.
     Johannesburg: South African Institute of
     Race Relations, 1983.   63 pp.

     James attempts to illustrate the various
     conditions under which the people of two homelands
     reside.

247. Moerdijk, Donald. Anti-Development, South Africa
     and Its Bantustans. Paris: UNESCO Press,
     1981.   194 pp.

     Moerdijk says that "This book outlines the
     process by which the apartheid government of the
     Republic of South Africa set out to maintain its
     policies by the fiction of 'independence' for its
     Bantustans."

248. Myers, Desaix, III.   "Impact of Apartheid:
     Constraints on Business."   Chapter II in U.S.
     Business in South Africa: The Economic,
     Political, and Moral Issues.   Bloomington:
     Indiana University Press, 1980.

     Myers describes the impact of apartheid on
     various aspects of South Africa's society such as
     land and housing, education of blacks, and
     business and labor.

249. The Plight of Black Women in Apartheid South
     Africa. New York: United Nations Department
     of Public Information, 1981.   35 pp.

250. Relocations: The Churches' Report on Forced
     Removals in South Africa. London: South
     African Council of Churches, 1984.   64 pp.

     Several leaders of Christian churches in
     South Africa examine the theories behind removal
     and relocations and the effects they have on the
     people.

251. Seedat, Aziza. Crippling a Nation: Health in
     Apartheid South Africa. Cambridge:
     International Defense and Aid Fund for
     Southern Africa, 1984. 110 pp.

252. Stultz, Newell M. Transkei's Half Loaf: Race
     Separatism in South Africa. New Haven: Yale
     University Press, 1979. 183 pp.

     Stultz addresses the question of whether
     independent states or homelands contribute to an
     increase in racial justice, lessen the change, or
     are not significant at all.

253. Wilson, Francis. South Africa: The Cordoned
     Heart. New York: W.W. Norton & Co., 1986.

     Wilson has compiled a series of photographs
     depicting poverty and the conditions of black
     women and children in the rural areas of South
     Africa.

254. Women Under Apartheid: In Photographs and Text.
     London: International Defense and Aid Fund
     for Southern Africa, 1981. 119 pp.

                        Articles

255. "Bantustanization in South Africa." Intl Affairs
     33 (June 5, 1982): 29-31.

     Discusses the government's policy of settling
     non-whites in separate geographic areas of the
     country from whites.

256. Benatar, S.R. "Medicine and Health Care in South
     Africa." New England J Med 315 (August 21,
     1986): 527-532.

     Benatar seeks to identify the shortcomings of
     the medical care system in that country.

257. Browne, F.H. "Mogopa: Death of a South African
        Village (Homelands Policy)." Chr Cent 101
        (April 11, 1984): 366-368.

        Browne looks at the effects of apartheid on
the living conditions of blacks in a South African
village.

258. Blyndell, John.   "Ciskei's Independent Way."
        Reason 16(April 1985): 22-33.

        The author examines the controversy
surrounding this black homeland. Some call Ciskei
a traitor regarding the fight against apartheid;
while others contend that it is a symbol of hope
for blacks in South Africa.

259. Daniels, Rudolph.   "The Nature of the Agrarian
        Land Question in the Republic of South
        Africa." Am J Econ Sociol 46 (January 1987):
        1-16.

        The author examines the distribution of land
in South Africa and how economics and race play a
major role in this problem.

260. Dugard, John.   "South Africa's Independent
        Homelands: An Exercise in
        Denationalization." Denver J Int L and Pol
        10(Fall 1980): 11-36.

261. Frankel, Philip.   "The Politics of Passes:
        Control and Change in South Africa." J Mod
        Afric Stud 17 (June, 1979): 199-218.

        The aim of this article is to demonstrate the
importance of the pass laws as a tool for the
white minority to maintain political domination
over the majority.

262. Grammon, Clive. "Swirling Shades of Gray."
     Sports Ill 58 (May 16, 1983): 78-84+.

     The author traces the history of sports in
     South Africa and examines the recent reforms in
     that country which allow blacks and whites to
     compete with each other.

263. Guttmacher, Sally. "Destructive Engagement: The
     Impact of Apartheid on Health Care in South
     Africa." Health/PAC Bull 16 (March/April
     1985): 9-15.

     Looks at the quality and quantity of delivery
     service and the overall health status of the
     country.

264. Hallett, Robin. "Desolation on the Veld: Forced
     Removals in South Africa." Afric Affairs 83
     (July 1984): 301-320.

     Hallett sees the system of apartheid as one
     that has developed into a unique feature of
     propaganda for the idea of social change that is
     really not changing for the betterment of all
     people.

265. Harsch, Ernest. "South Africa: Apartheid's Great
     Land Theft; How Racist System Keeps Blacks
     from Farming; A Revolution for Black Land
     Rights." Inter Pr 23 (December 16, 1985).
     752-759.

266. _____. "South Africa: The Plight of the Urban
     Squatter." Africa Rep 24 (May/June 1979):
     15-20.

     The author examines the reasons for and
     significance of the squatter camps and the role
     they play in the system of apartheid.

267. _____. "South Africa: Terror in the Bantustans;
     Black Quislings Carry Out Pretoria's Dirty
     Work." Inter Pr 21 (December 26, 1983): 754-
     755.

268. Hochschild, Adam. "Greene Is Detained. Yellow Is
     Missing. Red Is Confirmed Dead." Mother
     Jones 11 (September, 1986): 14+

     A journalist gives first-hand accounts on
     places, people, and situations he encountered in
     South Africa before the new state of emergency was
     imposed.

269. Howe, Russell W. "Facing the Inevitable in South
     Africa: Revolution and Partition." New
     Leader 68 (August 1985): 5-7.

     Howe considers some of the options that are
     available in order to bring an end to apartheid
     and the violence in South Africa.

270. Jeffrey, David. "Dilemma of Independence for
     South Africa's Ndebele People." Nat Geog 169
     (February 1986): 260-280.

     This article explores the significance of the
     Ndebele people getting independence in their
     homeland.

271. Klaaste, Aggrey. "Exiles in Their Native Land."
     NY Times M (June 24, 1984): 34-35+.

     The author describes the conditions that
     exist for the black miners in South Africa.

272. Lapchick, Richard E. "South Africa: Sport and
     Apartheid Politics." Am Academy Pol Soc
     Science 445 (September 1979): 155-165.

     Contends that sanctions from the
     international sports community have not brought
     about an end to apartheid in sports.

273. Mandela, Winnie, and Frense, Amina. "Winnie
     Mandela Interview." Ms 15 (January 1987):
     82-82, 100, 103.

In this interview, Mandela talks about the
effect that apartheid has on her country and her
hope for a better and peaceful life after the
dismantling of apartheid.

274. Mariechild, Jenna. "Fighting with Bare Hands."
     Comw 113 (February 28, 1986): 104-107.

     The author states that the homeland policy
was devised partly as an attempt to defuse world-
wide criticism of the apartheid system of racial
segregation.

275. Poinsette, Cheryl L. "Black Women Under
     Apartheid: An Introduction." Harv Women's
     Law J 8 (Spring 1985): 93-119.

     Poinsette contends that mechanisms and
controls of apartheid appear to be harsher on
women than on men.

276. "Republic of South Africa: Apartheid Enters Its
     Twilight Years." Africa Cont Rec 13
     (1980/81): B733-867.

     Covers an overview of the country's position
in the area of politics and economics. Also, what
is the outlook for the racial policies in South
Africa in the future?

277. "Terror in the Townships: A South Africa Update."
     AM Spectator 19 (July 1986): 22-25.

     Examines how the practice of apartheid has
brought about a climate of violence, particularly
for teenagers.

278. Treen, Joseph. "Apartheid's Harsh Grip."
     Newsweek 101 (March 28, 1983): 31-32+.

     Treen contends that "Botha's modest push for
reform has helped some blacks, but the majority
finds life worse than ever."

279. Tutu, Desmond. "Dismantling Apartheid." <u>Soc Educ</u>
     49:6 (September 1985): 453-456.

     Tutu discusses the true concept of apartheid
     in South Africa and suggests ways that
     countries and concerned individuals can bring an
     end to this system.

280. Waldorf, Lars. "Life in Crossroads." <u>New Repub</u>
     195 (August 25, 1986): 17-19.

     A white South African writes about life in
     the black townships.

                          Documents

281. U.N. General Assembly. A/AC. 115/L.551 Letter
     Dated 22 April 1981 from the Permanent
     Representative of Argentina to the United
     Nations Addressed to the Chairman of the
     Special Committee Against Apartheid. 8 June
     1981. 3 pp.

     Addresses visits by South African athletes to
     Argentina.

282. _____. A/AC. 115/L.609. Letters Relating to the
     English Rugby Football Union's Proposed Tour
     to South Africa. Special Committee Against
     Apartheid. 25 June 1984. 4 pp.

283. _____. A/Conf 94/BP/17. Reports of the
     Hemispheric Seminar on Women Under Apartheid,
     Montreal Canada, 9-11 May 1980 and the
     International Seminar on Women and Apartheid,
     Helsinki, Finland, 19-21 May 1980. 31 pp.

284. _____. E/CN.41/1497. Special Report of the Ad Hoc
            Working Group of Experts Prepared in
            Accordance With Commission on Human Rights
            Resolution and Economic and Social Council
            Resolution 1981/41. Study on the Effects of
            the Policy of Apartheid on Black Women and
            Children in South Africa. 8 January 1982. 26
            pp.

5.

EDUCATION

Monographs

285. Brewer, John D. "Soweto and Collective Action."
Chapter 1 in After Soweto: An Unfinished
Journey. New York: Clarendon Press, 1986.

Brewer talks about the inadequate education
system in South Africa and how apartheid has
brought on civil unrest in that country.

286. Education in South Africa: Conceptual Framework.
Washington: Information Counselor, South
African Embassy, 1980.

287. Education, Race, and Social Change in South
Africa. Berkeley: University of California
Press, 1982. 251 pp.

288. Finnegan, William. Crossing the Line: A Year in
the Land of Apartheid. New York: Harper &
Row Inc., 1986. 418 pp.

The author describes the unfairness
in the educational system in South Africa
and how the political system has helped to
maintain these inadequacies.

289. Harsch, Ernest. South Africa: White Rule, Black
Revolt. New York: Pathfinder Press, 1980.
352 pp.

In Chapter 8, the author says that the
government has adopted the Bantustan Program as a
means of controlling education, which would help
to maintain white supremacy.

290. Kallaway, Peter, ed. Apartheid and Education: The
      Education of Black South Africans. Athens:
      Ohio University Press, 1984. 496 pp.

291. Marcum, John A. Education, Race, and Social
      Change in South Africa. Berkeley:
      University of California Press, 1982.   251
      pp.

      Marcum and his team of American educators
examine the growing need of the government to
expand education of blacks in South Africa. Also,
the government's policy of apartheid as it relates
to education is discussed.

                          Articles

292. Charney, C. "Afrikaners Admit Blacks." Times
      Higher Educ Suppl no. 609 (July 6, 1984):   9.

      Charney looks at the stipulations that the
University of Potchefstroom has set for allowing
blacks to be admitted to its undergraduate
program.

293. _____. "New Racial Quotas Cause Anger Wave."
      Times Higher Educ Suppl no. 546 (April 22,
      1983): 7.

      The author reveals that several English-
speaking white universities are protesting the
current bill in Parliament that would limit the
number of black students that can enter these
universities.

294. _____. "University Referendum Says 'Yes' to
      Blacks on Campus." Times Higher Educ Suppl
      no. 523 (November 12, 1982): 7.

The author reports that students at the
conservative University of Pretoria voted to
endorse the university's decision to allow a small
number of black post-graduates for courses that
are not offered anywhere else.

295. _____. "Unrest Grows at Mixed Race University."
Times Higher Educ Suppl no. 484 (February 12,
1982): 8.

Charney examines the complaints that the
students at Western Cape University have
concerning the inferior teaching practices and
standards at this coloured university.

296. Chisholm, Linda. "Redefining Skills: Black
Education in South Africa in the 1980s."
Comp Educ 19:3 (1983): 357-71.

The author discusses the educational reforms
by the government and the impact of restructuring
racial division in technical training for blacks.

297. Christie, Pam. "Bantu Education: Apartheid
Ideology or Labour Reproduction." Comp Educ
18 (1982): 59-75.

The author interprets the various definitions
of the Bantu educational system. Most observers
contend that it is a system used to perpetuate
white domination over blacks.

298. Collins, Colin B. "Moving Education Forward to
Keep Society Back: The South African DeLange
Report Reevaluated." Comp Educ Rev, 28
(November 1984): 625-638.

Collins examines the educational system of
South Africa and talks about what changes should
be made in order to make the system an equal one
for blacks and whites.

299. Danaher, Kevin. "Educational Inequality in South
     Africa and Its Implications for U.S. Foreign
     Policy." Harvard Educ R 54 (May 1984): 166-
     174.

        Danaher argues that "the Reagan
     administration has attempted to justify its
     friendly relations with the white minority
     government of South Africa by claiming that
     apartheid is being reformed and that U.S.
     educational assistance is playing an important
     role in that process."

300. David, P. "Lull Before the Storm on Afrikaans
     Campuses." Times Higher Educ Suppl no. 377
     (January 11, 1980): 5.

        David believes that the higher education
     system in South Africa is closely related to the
     political ideology of that country and the
     students are becoming disenchanted with the
     current political system.

301. Dube, Ernest F. "The Relationship Between Racism
     and Education in South Africa." Harv Educ
     Rev 55:1 (February 1985): 86-100.

        Dube traces the correlation between
     apartheid and education in South Africa and the
     policies made by the government regarding this
     situation.

302. "Education and Social Control in South Africa."
     Afric Affairs (April 1979): 228-239.

303. Flather, P. "Apartheid Plays for Time." Times
     Higher Educ Suppl no. 480 (January 15, 1982):
     8.

        Flather reports on the outcome of the De
     Lange Report, which calls for opening all schools
     and universities to all races in South Africa.

304. Friedman, Helen. "Black Education in South
        Africa." Inter Educ 21 (January 1983): 3-92.

        In this article, Friedman says that the
     expenditure for education for blacks in South
     Africa is not as much as the other independent
     countries in Africa, even though South Africa's
     Gross Domestic Product is greater than any of
     these countries.

305. _____. "South Africa." Inter Educ 20:6
        (November-December 1983): 32-35.

        This article covers interviews conducted in
     South Africa with various individuals on the topic
     of black education and whether or not there is any
     improvement toward equal educational opportunity.

306. Garbers, Johang. "The Education Crisis in South
        Africa: Do Blacks Have the Training to Run
        the South African Economy?" Bus & Soc R
        (Fall 1986): 51-55.

        The author examines the effects of political
     change on education and the challenges confronting
     the education system in order to conform to a
     society after apartheid.

307. "International Education: Perspectives,
        Experiences, and Visions in an Interdependent
        World." Harv Educ R 55 (February 1985): 1-
        120.

        Part of this lengthy article identifies the
     relationship between education and racism in South
     Africa.

308. Johnson, Walton R. "Education: Keystone of
        Apartheid." Anthro Educ Q B (Fall 1982):
        214-237.

        Johnson says, "This paper is an analysis of
     the relationship of education to the system of
     apartheid in South Africa. It explores the manner

in which education is being manipulated to
maintain a system of social stratification based
upon race, ethnic background and language."

309. Kane-Berman, J.   "Vista Shows Apartheid Will
     Continue."   Times Educ Suppl no. 3399 (August
     21, 1981): 9.

     The author reports that the establishment of
     another separate university for blacks, to be
     known as Vista University, is a continuing sign of
     the unequal system of education under the system
     of apartheid.

310. "No Place For the African: South Africa's
     Education System, Meant to Bolster Apartheid,
     May Destroy It."   Index on Censorship 10
     (October 1981): 79.

311. "Progressives Hope for Apartheid Policy Shift."
     Times Higher Educ Suppl no. 412 (September
     26, 1980): 6.

     Calls for an inquiry into the inequality of
     higher education in South Africa and demands that
     something be done to bring an end to this
     practice.

312. Randolph-Robinson, Brenda.   "The Depiction of
     South Africa in U.S. Textbooks."   Black Sch 6
     (November/December 1985): 24-33.

     The author feels that there is some
     distortion in the textbooks as to how the
     system of apartheid really works in South Africa.

313. Simon, Alan.   "Black Students' Perceptions of
     Factors Related to Academic Performance in a
     Rural Area of Natal Province, South Africa."
     J Negro Educ 55 (Fall 1986): 535-547.

314. "South Africa in Crisis." <u>Times Higher Educ Suppl</u>
     no. 694 (February 21, 1986): 14-15.

     Reviews the effects of the state of emergency
     on the students at the universities in South
     Africa.

315. Wilce, H. "Why Pupils Rioted and Left School."
     <u>Times Educ Suppl</u> no. 3521 (December 23,
     1983): 10.

     Wilce details the remarks of two young black
     South Africans about their experiences in seeking
     an education under the system of apartheid.

316. Zille, H. "Many Blame Separate and Unequal
     Education for Poor Test Scores of South
     Africa Blacks." <u>Chron Higher Educ</u> 27
     (January 25, 1984): 27.

     The author states that many educators claim
     that the pass and failure rate of students is in
     many ways directly related to the amount of money
     spent by the government on black and white
     students.

317. _____. "South Africa's English-Language
     Universities Balk at Enforcing Quota System
     for Blacks." <u>Chron Higher Educ</u> 26 (June 29,
     1983): 21.

     The author examines the confrontation
     developing between five English-language
     universities and the government over a bill
     establishing a quota system for blacks being
     admitted in the area of higher education.

Documents

318. Dean, Elizabeth. <u>History in Black and White: An</u>
     <u>Analysis of South African School History</u>
     <u>Textbooks</u>. Washington, D.C.: Educational
     Resources Information Center, 1983.   137 pp.
     (ED248185).

     Dean examines the way different ethnic groups
     are depicted in South African school history
     textbooks. The majority of the representations of
     these groups were done through myths and
     stereotyping.

319. U.N. General Assembly. UNST/PSCA (05)/N911.
     Education For Blacks in South Africa:
     Deconstructing the Myths. Secretariat.
     Department of Political and Security Council
     Affairs. Centre Against Apartheid. October
     1986. 26 pp.

6.

RELIGION

Monographs

320. Boesak, Allan Aubrey. <u>Black and Reformed:</u>
<u>Apartheid, Liberation, and the Calvinist</u>
<u>Tradition</u>. New York: Orbis, 1984. 167 pp.

Boesak presents a collection of addresses
between 1974 and 1983 reflecting on the
experiences of black South Africans and their
resistance to the all-white government.

321. _____. <u>Comfort and Protest</u>. Philadelphia:
Westminister Press, 1987.

Pages 10-12 reveal certain aspects about
Boesak's fight to end apartheid in South Africa.

322. _____. <u>The Finger of God: Sermons on Faith and</u>
<u>Responsibility</u>. New York: Orbis Books,
1982. 100 pp.

The author's sermons all have the same theme
in that they address the social and political
responsibility of all Christians in South Africa.

323. _____. When Prayer Makes News. Philadelphia:
     Westminister Press, 1986.

     Boesak and others examine the use of prayers
     in the various churches throughout South Africa to
     protest against the current government in that
     country.

324. Carter, Gwendolyn M. Which Way Is South Africa
     Going? Bloomington: Indiana University
     Press, 1980. 162 pp.

     From pages 103-110 Carter discusses the
     powerful role that religion plays in providing the
     philosophy and justification of white South
     African actions. Also, she elaborates on the
     development of the black theology and its doctrine
     of self-pride and self-confidence.

325. Davies, Robert H. The Struggle for South Africa:
     A Reference Guide to Movements, Organization,
     and Institutions. London: Zed Books, 1984.
     440 pp. Vol. II.

     On pages 273-276 Davies discusses the
     church's ideology in regard to apartheid.

326. DeGruchy, John W. The Church's Struggle in South
     Africa. Grand Rapids: W.B. Eerdmans, 1986.
     290 pp.

     DeGruchy attempts to explain the influence
     the church has on both blacks and whites in
     directing their actions toward the social and
     political conditions of that country.

327. _____. Cry Justice: Prayers, Meditations, and
     Readings from South Africa. New York: Orbis
     Books, 1986. 261 pp.

328. Hope, Marjorie. The South African Churches in a
     Revolutionary Situation. New York: Orbis
     Books, 1981.

329. Mosala, Itumeleng J., ed. The Unquestionable
     Right to Be Free: Black Theology from South
     Africa. New York: Orbis Books, 1986. 206
     pp.

     The author has compiled a series of essays
     addressing the South African black struggle
     against the white government of that country.

330. Tutu, Desmond. The Divine Intention. Braam
     Fontein: South African Council of Churches, 1982.
     38 pp.

331. _____. Hope and Suffering: Sermons and Speeches.
     Johannesburg: Skotaville Publishers, 1983.
     149 pp.

332. Walshe, Peter. Church Versus State in South
     Africa: The Case of the Christian Institute.
     London: C. Hurst and Co., 1983. 234 pp.

     The author attempts to show how a Dutch
     Reformed clergyman tried to convince fellow
     Afrikaners that apartheid was and still is un-
     christian.

333. War and Conscience in South Africa: The Churches
     and Conscientious Objection. London:
     Catholic Institute for International
     Relations, 1982. 112 pp.

                        Articles

334. Barkat, Anwar M. "Churches Combating Racism in
     South Africa." J Int Aff 36 (Fall/Winter
     1982/83): 297-305.

     Barkat describes how the World Council has
     helped to expose the origin of apartheid and its
     effect upon the lives of black South Africans.

335. Brouwer, Arie and Castro, Emilio. "Church Groups
     Lead the Battle Against Apartheid." Bus &
     Soc R (Spring 1986): 106-112.

Brouwer talks about the effort of the
National Council of Churches of Christ's fight
against the system of apartheid and what they are
doing and trying to encourage other groups to do.

336. Crapanzano, Vincent. "Waiting (II)." NY 61
     (March 25, 1985): 52-54+.

The author examines the Dutch Reformed
Churches and their strong approval of the
institution of apartheid.

337. Dempster, C. "Theological Apartheid Clash."
     Times Higher Educ Suppl no. 600 (May 4,
     1984): 9.

Dempster reveals that about one hundred
students have boycotted the University of the
Western Cape because the lecturers are members of
the Reformed Church that finds apartheid to be in
harmony with the Bible.

338. DuToit, A. "Puritans in Africa? Afrikaner
     'Calvinism' and Kuyperian neo-Calvinism in
     Late Nineteenth Century South Africa." Comp
     Stud Soc Hist 27 (April 1985): 209-240.

The author says that Calvinism has been used
as a method of trying to explain the ideology of
apartheid and Afrikaner Nationalism.

339. Earley, Pete. "Desmond Tutu: God and the
     Politics of Commitment." Wash Post M
     (February 16, 1986): 8-11, 13, 15-17.

Discusses Tutu's remarks on such topics as
politics, religion and apartheid.

340. Green, C. J. "South African Church Leaders Speak
     Out." Chr and Crisis 45 (November 11, 1985):
     440-444.

The author states that key church members and
leaders in South Africa signed the Kairos Document
condemning the system of apartheid.

341. Hexham, Irving. "Dutch Calvinism and the
     Development of Afrikaner Nationalism." Afric
     Affairs 79 No. 315 (1980): 195-208.

     Hexham talks about the early development and
philosophical theme of the Dutch Reformed Church
and how this development helped shape Afrikaners'
way of thinking in regard to race.

342. Hurley, Archbishop Denis. "South Africa: The
     Catholic Church and Apartheid." Africa Rep
     28:4 (July-August 1983): 17-19.

     Hurley speaks about the Catholic Church's
responsibility to its black and white members and
how they approach the system of apartheid.

343. Mzimela, Sipo E. "Nazism and Apartheid: The Role
     of the Christian Churches in Nazi Germany and
     Apartheid South Africa." New York
     University, DAI, 1981, 43, 2436A.

     Mzimela examines the possibility of whether a
Confessing Church can bring an end to apartheid in
South Africa.

344. Nunnelee, Randy. "South Africa's Prisoners of
     Hope." America 152 (January 19, 1985): 48-
     50.

     The author says that "More and more, the
churches of South Africa, their leaders and
members are standing in solidarity with the
struggles of the oppressed black majority in South
Africa."

345. "South Africa: Can the Church Mend the Anguish of
     a Nation?" Christ Tod 30 (November 21,
     1986): 1-I-19-I.

     This article discusses the findings of a
research team in South Africa investigating the
role of the church in its fight to end civil and
social unrest.

346. Strauss, Pieter J. "Relations Between the Dutch
     Reformed Church and the Reformed Churches in
     the Netherlands with Regard to the South
     African Racial Issue." University of
     Pretoria, DAI, 1985, 45, 2563-A.

     Strauss believes that the Dutch Reformed
Church based and supported apartheid on the
teachings in the Bible.

347. "White Theology's Last Bastion." Time 113
     (January 1, 1979): 69+.

     This article examines the growing discontent
of the Dutch Reformed Churches and their practice
of racial segregation in South Africa.

348. Williams, Oliver F. "The Religious Rationale of
     Racism: The Role of the Dutch Reformed
     Church in South Africa." Bus & Soc R (Spring
     1986): 101-105.

     Williams gives a brief history of the DRC and
its current ideology for rationalizing their
support for the system of apartheid.

7.

WORLD VIEWS

Monographs

349. Agbogun, Jacob B. "Sport and Politics: The
Stance of Nigeria on the South African
Apartheid Policy in Sports, 1960-1982," Ph.D.
diss. University of Alberta (Canada), 1983.

350. Anzovin, Steven. South Africa: Apartheid and
Divestiture. New York: H.W. Wilson Co,
1987.

This book contains a series of articles,
excerpts from books and addresses on current
issues regarding the problems in South Africa and
what can be done to bring an end to apartheid.

351. Apartheid Under Siege: The U.S. and South Africa
-- 1985. Durham: Africa News Service, 1985.
35 pp.

352. Baker, James E., and O'Flaherty, J. Full Report:
Public Opinion Poll of American Attitudes
Towards South Africa. New York: Carnegie
Endowment for International Peace, 1979. 42
pp.

353. Baldwin, Brooke, and Brown, Theodore. Economic
Action Against Apartheid: An Analysis of the
Divestment Campaign and Financial
Implications for Institutional Investors.
New York: The Africa Fund, 1985. 47 pp.

The author says, "This report will address
the question of what constitutes that corporate
presence and why its supporters now perceive the
threat of the divestment campaign to be so great
as to require an increased and increasingly public
defense."

354. Bissell, Richard E. South Africa and the United
     States: The Erosion of an Influence
     Relationship. New York: Praeger, 1982. 147
     pp.

     Bissell details the relationship between the
     U.S. and South Africa from a political, strategic,
     economic, and cultural point of view.

355. Blumenfeld, Jesmond, ed. South Africa in Crisis.
     London: Croom Helm Ltd., 1987. 207 pp.

     Blumenfeld examines the economic and social
     changes of the white government of South Africa
     and their overall policy of apartheid.

356. Bok, Derek. Beyond the Ivory Tower: Social
     Responsibilities of the Modern University.
     Cambridge, Mass.: Harvard University Press,
     1982.

     On pages 289-293 Bok examines the potential
     of universities divesting stocks in an attempt to
     bring about an end to apartheid in South Africa.

357. Brehme, Gerhard, ed. Apartheid: Mass Violation
     of Human Rights. New York: VCH Publishers,
     Inc., 1980. 106 pp.

     This covers the results of a symposium on
     apartheid held at the Karl Marx University in
     Germany. Several contributors express their views
     on the racial policies of South Africa.

357a. Bryant, Coralie, ed. Poverty, Policy, and Food
      Security in Southern Africa. Boulder: Lynne
      Rienner Publishers, 1988. 291 pp.

In Chapter 9, several black South African leaders give their views of the U.S. policy toward South Africa.

358. Butler, Stuart M. An Investment Strategy to Undermine Apartheid in South Africa. Washington: Heritage Foundation, 1985. 11 pp.

359. Chazam, Naomi. "The Fallacies of Pragmatism: Israeli Foreign Policy Toward South Africa." Jews in Black Perspectives. Edited by Joseph R. Washington. Cranbury, N.J.: Associated University Press, 1984, pp. 148-181.

The author examines the relationship between these two countries and the debates surrounding it.

359a. Haego, Chen. "Commonwealth: Fight Against Apartheid Strengthened." Beijing R 31(February 15, 1988): 16-17.

360. Christenson, Philip L. "United States-South African Economic Relations: Major Issues in the United States." The American People and South Africa. Edited by Alfred O. Hero, Jr. Lexington: D. C. Heath Co., 1981, pp. 47-65.

Christenson feels that economic sanctions are unlikely to have any major impact of encouraging domestic reform in South Africa.

361. Clarke, D. G. Economic Sanctions on South Africa: Past Evidence and Future Potential. Geneva: International University Exchange Fund, 1980. 35 pp.

362. Clarke, Simon. Financial Aspects of Economic Sanctions on South Africa. Geneva: International University Exchange Fund, 1980. 126 pp.

363. Coffe, Mary Lee. "The Development of the United
        States Divestiture Movement and Its Impact on
        Apartheid on South Africa." Ph.D. diss.
        Howard University, 1986.

364. Coker, Christopher. The United States and South
        Africa, 1968-1985: Constructive Engagement
        and Its Critics. North Carolina: Duke
        University Pr., 1986. 327 pp.

        Based on a Ph.D. thesis that looks at the
     U.S. policy of ending apartheid through positive
     sanctions.

365. Congressional Quarterly Almanac. Washington,
        D.C.: Congressional Quarterly, Inc., 1985,
        Vol. 41, pp. 83-90.

        Congress forces the President to impose
     economic and political sanctions against the South
     African government.

366. Congressional Quarterly Almanac. Washington,
        D.C.: Congressional Quarterly, Inc., 1985,
        Vol. 41, pp. 39-40.

        Several members of Congress criticize
     Reagan's policy of constructive engagement and
     call for tougher measures of sanctions to deal
     with South Africa and its racial policies.

367. Congressional Quarterly Almanac. Washington,
        D.C.: Congressional Quarterly, Inc., 1986,
        Vol. 42, pp. 359-373.

        The Senate overrides Reagan's veto of
     measures (HR 4868) that would impose economic
     sanctions against South Africa.

368. Omitted.

369. Davies, Rob J. <u>Trade Sanctions and the Regional</u>
     <u>Impact in Southern Africa</u>. Geneva:
     International University Exchange Fund, 1980.
     37 pp.

        Davies talks about economic repercussions
     that could develop for the southern region of
     Africa if sanctions are placed against South
     Africa.

370. Deats, Paul. "U.S. Religious Institutions and
     South Africa." <u>The American People and South</u>
     <u>Africa</u>. Edited by Alfred O. Hero, Jr.
     Lexington: D.C. Heath Co., 1981, pp. 103-122.

        Deats examines the opinions of U.S. church
     leaders on the subject of economic and political
     change in South Africa.

371. <u>Disinvestment: Is It Legal? Is It Moral? Is It</u>
     <u>Productive</u>? Washington, D.C.: National
     Legal Center for the Public Interest, 1985.
     109 pp.

        Several authors discuss the pros and cons of
     disinvestment and what it means to South Africa
     and the rest of the world.

372. <u>The Divestment of Ohio Public Pension Funds in</u>
     <u>U.S. Companies Which Do Business in South</u>
     <u>Africa</u>. Columbus: Ohio Retirement Study
     Commission, 1983. 40 pp.

373. Elliot, Charles. <u>The International Impact and</u>
     <u>Adjustment to Economic Sanctions on South</u>
     <u>Africa</u>. Geneva: International University
     Exchange Fund, 1980. 32 pp.

374. Farina, Linda. <u>Assessing the Impact of Economic</u>
     <u>Sanctions on Black Welfare in South Africa</u>.
     Geneva: International University Exchange
     Fund, 1980. 32 pp.

375. Fisher, Scott. Coping with Change: United States
     Policy Toward South Africa. Washington,
     D.C.: National Defense University Press,
     1982. 83 pp.

376. Gayner, J. B. The Choice for U.S. Policy in South
     Africa: Reform or Vengeance. Washington,
     D.C.: Heritage Foundation, 1986. 11 pp.

     Indicates that the President of the United
     States has called for sanctions against South
     Africa in its fight to end apartheid.

377. Geldenhuys, D.J. Sanctions Against South Africa.
     Johannesburg: South African Institute of
     International Affairs, 1979. 27 pp.

377a. Hammarskjold, Dag. Sanctions Against South
      Africa: A Selective Bibliography. New York.
      United Nations, 1981. 28 pp.

378. Haslam, David. The Campaign Against Bank Loans
     for Apartheid. New York: U.N. Centre
     Against Apartheid. United Nations, 1979. 8
     pp.

379. Hauch, David. Two Decades of Debate: The
     Controversy Over U.S. Companies in South
     Africa. Washington: Investor Responsibility
     Research Center, 1983. 163 pp.

380. Hero, Alfred O., ed. The American People and
     South Africa: Publics, Elite and Policy-
     Making Processes. Lexington, MA: Lexington
     Books, 1981, 229 pp.

381. International Labour Office. International Labour
     Conference: 67th Session, 1981: Tenth Item
     on the Application of the Declaration
     Concerning the Policy of Apartheid of the
     Republic of South Africa. Geneva:
     International Labour Office, 1981. 102 pp.

382. International Labour Office. International Labour
          Conference: 69th Session, 1983: Special
          Report of the Director-General on the
          Application of the Declaration Concerning the
          Policy of Apartheid in South Africa. Geneva:
          International Labour Office, 1983. 127 pp.

383. International Labour Organization. Special Report
          on the Application of the Declaration
          Concerning the Policy of Apartheid in South
          Africa. Geneva: International Labour
          Office, 1985. 209 pp.

          Talks about the recent developments in labour
     and social aspects in South Africa and what
     international organizations are trying to do to
     bring an end to apartheid.

383a. Klinghoffer, Arthur Jay. Oiling the Wheels of
          Apartheid: Exposing South Africa's Secret
          Oil Trade. Boulder: Lynne Rienner Pubs.,
          1989.

384. Kitchen, Helen, ed. Options for U. S. Policy
          Toward Africa. Washington: American
          Enterprise Institute for Public Policy
          Research, 1979. 76 pp.

385. Kitchen, Helen, and Clough, Michael. The United
          States and South Africa: Realities and Red
          Herrings. Washington: Center for Strategic
          and International Studies, 1984.

386. Leape, Jonathan, ed. Business in the Shadow of
          Apartheid: U.S. Firms in South Africa.
          Lexington, MA: Lexington Books, 1985. 242
          pp.

387. Litvak, Lawrence, and DeGrasse, Robert. South
          Africa: Foreign Investment and Apartheid.
          Washington: Institute for Policy Studies,
          1979. 104 pp.

388. Love, Janice. The U.S. Anti-Apartheid Movement:
        Local Activism in Global Politics. New York:
        Praeger Pub., 1985. 296 pp.

     The author examines the steps taken by non-
     governmental groups in their efforts to change
     government and business policies toward South
     Africa.

389. Minty, A.S. "The Anti-Apartheid Movement and
     Racism in South Africa." Pressure Groups in the
     Global System. Edited by P. Willetts. New York:
     St. Martin's Press, 1982, pp. 28-45.

     The author describes how the Anti-Apartheid
     Movement, a non-governmental organization, works
     towards its main goal of bringing an end to
     apartheid.

390. Morrell, Jim. International Institutions and
        Economic Sanctions on South Africa. Geneva:
        International University Exchange Fund, 1980.
        38 pp.

391. Myers, Desaix, III. "The Controversy Over
        Sanctions Against South Africa." Chapter VI
        in U.S. Business in South Africa: The
        Economic, Political and Moral Issues.
        Bloomington: Indiana University Press, 1980.

     Myers examines all the ramifications
     involving the issues of sanctions and the U.S.
     policy toward South Africa in the areas of
     investments and sales.

392. _____. "U.S. Domestic Controversy over American
        Business in South Africa." The American
        People and South Africa. Edited by Alfred O.
        Hero, Jr. Lexington: D.C. Heath Co., 1981,
        pp. 67-82.

     Myers confirms that the system of economic
     pressures by students and concerned citizens in
     the U.S. against South Africa is in place and well
     established.

393. Oil and Apartheid: Churches' Challenge to Shell
     and BP. London: Christian Concern for
     Southern Africa, March 1982. 78 pp.

394. Perceptions of Western Attitudes to South Africa:
     Three Views. Johannesburg: South African
     Institute of International Affairs, July
     1980. 10 pp.

395. Pifer, Alan. South Africa in the American Mind.
     Johannesburg: South African Institute of
     International Affairs, 1981. 17 pp.

396. Razis, Vic. The American Connection: The
     Influence of United States Business on South
     Africa. New York: St. Martin's Pr., 1986,
     246 pp.

     Razis talks about "effects of the American
     multinational corporation on South African
     economic growth and political reform. This is
     also concerned with related issues such as
     American policy towards South African trade, bank
     loans, and the racial and cultural impact of the
     American presence."

397. Reagan, Ronald. Ending Apartheid in South Africa.
     Washington, D.C.: U.S. Dept. of State,
     Bureau of Public Affairs, 1986. 4 pp.

     Reagan states that "This administration is
     not only against broad economic sanctions and
     against apartheid; we are for a new South Africa,
     a new nation where all that has been built up over
     generations is not destroyed, a new society where
     participation in the social, cultural, and
     political life is open to all people."

398. Riddell, Roger. Economic Sanctions and the South
     African Agricultural Sector. Geneva:
     International University Exchange Fund, 1980.
     42 pp.

399. Rotberg, Robert I. "Confronting the Common
     Danger: South Africa and the United States
     in the Reagan Era." The American People and
     South Africa. Edited by Alfred O. Hero, Jr.
     Lexington: D.C. Heath Co., 1981, pp. 201-215.

     Rotberg contends that the Reagan
     administration has an opportunity to wipe out the
     spread of Marxism in southern Africa by demanding
     significant change and negotiation among the
     blacks and whites of that country.

400. _____. Suffer the Future: Policy Choices in
     Southern Africa. Cambridge, Mass.: Harvard
     University Press, 1980. 311 pp.

     Rotberg examines the physical and social
     fundamentals of South Africa.

401. Seidman, Ann. Economic Sanctions as a Basic
     Choice in Southern Africa. Geneva:
     International University Exchange Fund, 1980.
     32 pp.

402. Shultz, George. The U.S. Approach to South
     Africa. Washington: U.S. Dept. of State,
     Bureau of Public Affairs, 1986. 6 pp.

     The Secretary of State explains the
     President's stand on apartheid and his call for
     all South Africans to work toward an end to
     abolishing apartheid.

403. Sincere, Richard, Jr. The Politics of Sentiment:
     Churches and Foreign Investment in South
     Africa. Washington, D.C.: Ethics and Public
     Policy Center, 1984.

     Sincere says of this book, "It is a study of
     whether foreign investment in South Africa helps
     or hinders the course of greater justice for the
     people of all races there."

404. South Africa and Sanctions: Genesis and
          Prospects. Symposium, Johannesburg, 1979.
          Papers and Comments. Johannesburg: South
          African Institute of Race Relations and South
          African Institute of International Affairs,
          1979, pp. 71-79.

405. Spandau, Arnt. Economic Boycott Against South
          Africa. Kenwyn: Juta, 1979.

          Spandau examines whether an external trade
     boycott can be considered a suitable means of
     persuading the government of South Africa to
     relinquish its policy of racial discrimination.

406. Special Report of the Director-General on the
          Application of the Declaration Concerning the
          Policy of Apartheid in South Africa. Geneva:
          International Labour Office, 1987. 180 pp.

407. Sports and Apartheid: Caribbean Sports People and
          The Boycott of South Africa. Barbados:
          Southern Africa Liberation Committee, 1983.
          24 pp.

408. Stultz, Newell M. Foreign Pressures on South
          Africa. Hanover, N.H.: American
          Universities Field Staff, 1981. 11 pp.

409. Study Commission on U.S. Policy Toward Southern
          Africa. South Africa: Time Running Out.
          Berkeley: University of California Press,
          1981. 517 pp.

          Contains information covered in a two-year
     study and hearing examining the political, social,
     and economic conditons of that country.

410. Sullivan, Leon Howard. The Role of Multinational
          Corporations in South Africa: The 1980
          Hoernle Memorial Lecture. Johannesburg:
          South African Institute of Race Relations,
          1980. 25 pp.

411. Tucker, Robert W. <u>Intervention and The Reagan
     Doctrine</u>. New York: The Council on Religion
     and International Affairs, 1985. 30 pp.

412. Vander Bent, Ans J., ed. <u>Breaking Down the Walls:
     World Council of Churches Statements and
     Actions on Racism, 1948-1985</u>. Geneva: World
     Council of Churches, 1986. 107 pp.

412a. Wallish, Jim. <u>Crucible of Fire: The Church
     Confronts Apartheid</u>. Maryknoll: Orbis
     Books, 1989.

413. Williams, Oliver F. <u>The Apartheid Crisis: How We
     Can Do Justice in a Land of Violence</u>. San
     Francisco: Harper & Row, 1986. 124 pp.

     The author argues for maintaining a business
relationship with South Africa, which would allow
the outside community the opportunity to improve
the conditions of blacks in that country.

                        Articles

414. Abdul-Rahim, Salih. "Washington's Growing
     Alliance with Apartheid." <u>So Africa</u> 16:2
     (March 1983): 17-18.

     The author cites several examples of the
Reagan Administration's policy changes toward
South Africa.

415. Abegunrin, Olayinola. "The Arabs and the Southern
     African Problem." <u>Intl Affairs</u> 60:1 (Winter
     1983-1984): 97-105.

     The author examines the ties between Arab and
African states and their fight to end racism in
South Africa.

416. Adelman, K. "Western Policy in Southern Africa."
     <u>Curr Hist</u> (March 1980): 124-126.

Adelman feels that western pressure helped to
bring about domestic reforms in South Africa and
that more and more white South Africans are
beginning to realize that they must adapt to these
changes.

417. "Africa, The United States, and South Africa."
     Africa Rep 27 (September/October 1982): 10-
     13.

     The article calls for the use of sanctions by
     the United States as a means of ending or
     dismantling apartheid.

418. "America and South Africa." Economist 294 (March
     30, 1985): 17-22, 25-34.

     The recent attack and killing by South
     African police of 19 people has weakened Reagan's
     policy of "constructive engagement."

419. Amerongen, Otto Wolf Von. "Economic Sanctions as
     a Foreign Policy Tool?" Int Sec 5: 2 (Fall
     1980): 159-167.

     The author contends that sanctions must be
     the last resort to be considered if political or
     diplomatic measures do not work.

420. "The Anti-Apartheid Movement and the Populist
     Instinct in American Politics." Polit Sci Q
     101:3 (1986): 379-395.

     This article examines the origin of the anti-
     apartheid movement in the U.S. and the role it has
     played in American politics and influencing public
     support on the issue of apartheid.

421. Antilla, S. "Socially Responsible Investments."
     Work Wom 10 (April 1985): 38+.

422. "Apartheid and the United Nations." R Internat
     Affairs 33 (April 20, 1982): 20-22.

The author covers the relationship between
the U.N. General Assembly and the problem of
apartheid from its very beginnings in the 1940's.

423. "Apartheid Protests Begin to Bite." Times Higher
     Educ Suppl no. 677 (October 25, 1985): 10.

     This article examines the protests and
     demonstrations by U.S. students on the various
     campuses against the system of apartheid in South
     Africa.

424. Armacost, Michael H. "Promoting Positive Change
     in Southern Africa." Dept State Bul 86
     (April 1986): 49-53.

     Armacost examines such topics as the pros and
     cons of disinvestment and the importance of the
     Sullivan Principles in bringing an end to
     apartheid.

425. Ashford, Nicholas. "South Africa and the Threat
     of Economic Sanctions." Optima 28, No. 3
     (August 1979): 139-151.

     The author outlines the pros and cons of
     economic sanctions and what effect, if any, they
     will have on South Africa's economy.

426. Asoyan, B. "South Africa: The Apartheid System
     Is Doomed." Intl Affairs (November 1985):
     53-59.

     The author makes critical comments concerning
     the relationship between the U.S. government and
     that of South Africa.

427. "Assembly Approves Three Global Meetings on
     Southern Africa Issues; Adopts International
     Convention Against Apartheid in Sports." UN
     Chron 23 (February 1986): 16-25.

     This article examines the General Assembly's
     decision to hold meetings on the subjects of
     apartheid and sanctions against South Africa.

428. Baade, Robert A., and Galloway, Jonathan.
      "Economic Sanctions Against the Union of
      South Africa: Policy Options." <u>Alternatives</u>
      4: 4 (1979): 487-505.

429. Baker, Donald G. "South African Policy and U.S.
      Responses." <u>Intl Affairs Bull</u> 3: 2 (1979):
      27-46.

430. Baker, James E. "The American Consensus on South
      Africa." <u>Worldview</u> 22 (October 1979): 12-16.

431. Baker, Pauline H. "Facing up to Apartheid."
      <u>Foreign Pol</u> 64 (Fall 1986): 37-62.

      The author feels that the U.S. policy toward
      South Africa is much too passive in ending
      apartheid. Also, she explains that this weak
      policy will eventually lead to strained race
      relations in the U.S.

432. Barber, James. "Sanctions Against South Africa --
      Options for the West." <u>Intl Affairs</u> 55
      (July 1979): 385-401.

      Barber discusses the various options that
      exist for the western states planning on imposing
      sanctions on South Africa. These countries will
      probably impose sanctions within the three central
      lines of policy which are communication,
      disengagement and pressure for reform.

433. Barron, Deborah D. "The Public Views South
      Africa: Pathways Through a Gathering Storm."
      <u>Pub Opin</u> (January, February 1979): 54-59.

434. Battersby, John. "Thatcher's Gamble." <u>Africa Rep</u>
      31 (July-August 1986): 4-8.

      A group visiting South Africa from the
      Commonwealth returns with an endorsement of
      sanctions against South Africa.

435. Beaty, David, and Harari, Oren. "Divestment and
      Disinvestment from South Africa: A

Reappraisal." <u>Cal Manag R</u> 29 (Summer 1987): 31-50.

The authors contend that American firms should base their decisions on disengagement of South Africa businesses from a moral view.

436. Beaubien, Michael C. "The Cultural Boycott of South Africa." <u>Afr Today</u> 29:4 (1982): 5-16.

Beaubien describes the situation that American artists are being confronted with in regard to their performances in South Africa.

437. Becker, Charles M. "Economic Sanctions Against South Africa." <u>Wld Pol J</u> 39 (January 1987): 147-173.

Becker contends that the proper sanctions will be the least likely to harm South Africa's black population.

438. Belfiglio, Valentine J. "Strategic Importance of South Africa to the United States." <u>Africa Insight</u> 10: 2 (1980): 81-86.

Belfiglio discusses the different options on which the U.S. could structure its foreign policy toward South Africa without bringing any major boycotts into play.

438a. Biermann, John. "The Challenge to Sanctions." <u>Macl Mag</u> 102 (March 13, 1989): 24+.

439. Bochkaryov, Yuri. "Bankruptcy of the Apartheid Regime." <u>New Times</u> no. 33 (August 1985): 18-21.

440. Bokembya, Nkanga. "An Ethical Analysis of United States Policy Toward South Africa (Politics, Ethics, Moral Tradition, National Interest, Apartheid, Covenantal Norms)." Vanderbilt University, <u>DAI</u>, 1984, 46: 2323-A.

Bokembya contends that U.S. policy toward
South Africa contradicts its own moral
tradition. Also, the author feels that the main
change in U.S. policy should be directed toward
human rights violations in that country.

441. Bradlee, Ben, Jr. "Taking Sides on South Africa."
     Boston Globe Mag (February 24, 1985): 8-12,
     46-47, 53, 55-58, 60-61.

The author examines the debate taking place
in the U.S. of whether their investments in
South Africa help or hurt the system of apartheid.

442. "Breaking the Engagement: Congress Has Run out of
     Patience with South Africa, and that Has
     Forced President Reagan to Back Away from His
     Policy of Constructive Engagement." Natl J
     18 (July 26, 1986): 1820-1824.

443. "Britain's Goodbye?" Maclean's 99 (August 18,
     1986): 2, 14-22.

Prime Minister Thatcher refuses to go along
with the 11 economic sanctions imposed by the
Commonwealth leaders on South Africa.

444. Brouwer, Arie R. "Church Groups Lead the Battle
     Against Apartheid." Bus & Soc R (Spring
     1986): 106-112.

Brouwer indicates that the U.S. Council of
churches hopes that the instituting of sanctions
would help prevent a civil war in South Africa and
that freedom and peace will eventually come to
that country.

445. Brown, Frank Dexter. "Amandla! The Rallying Cry
     Against Apartheid." Black Enterp 15 (April
     1985): 58-61.

Due to increasing incidents of death and
illegal detention of blacks in South Africa, there
appears to be a strong antiapartheid movement
growing in the U.S.

446. Brunson, Paul M. "Investment in South Africa: A
     Challenge to Schools of Social Work." Soc
     Work 25 (July 1980): 315-317.

     Brunson has attempted to question the
     apparent hypocrisy between social work values and
     certain practices regarding investment in South
     Africa.

447. Bryan, Sam, ed. "Focus on South Africa: Time
     Running Out." Intercom, no. 105   (November
     1983): 6-54.

448. "The Case Against South Africa." Ebony 40 (May
     1985): 132-4+.

     Randall Robinson and Edward Kennedy express
     their views on the issues of apartheid and call on
     the U.S. to apply sanctions against South Africa
     as a means to end the system of racial separation.

449. Cason, Jim, and Fleshman, Mike.   "Profit Without
     Honor; Divesting from Apartheid." Chr and
     Crisis 46 (June 16, 1986): 212-217.

     The authors contend that the South African
     economy would suffer a crippling blow if it were
     deprived of the loans, products, and the contacts
     supplied by the United States.

450. Cavin, Tony. "What Oil Embargo?" South Africa
     14: 3 (May, June 1981): 11, 30-31.

451. Chettle, John.   "Is There any Justification for
     Economic Pressure Against South Africa?"
     Issue 9: 1,2 (1979): 24-29.

     Chettle concludes that improvement in the
     current racial situation in South Africa can best
     be handled by imploring U.S. corporations to
     improve the conditions of their employees and to
     ensure that they are all treated with equality.
     He concludes that this would be a more effective
     means than economic sanctions.

452._____. "The United States and South Africa:
            Barriers to Communication." Orbis 25 (Spring
            1981): 145-163.

        Chettle feels that with a new administration
taking over in the U.S. it is more likely that
South Africa will now be encouraged more than it
was condemned.

453. "Closer Ties with South Africa --- U.S. Gain at
      High Cost." U.S. News World Rep 91
      (September 21, 1981): 39+.

        Robin Knight, chief of the magazine's Africa
Bureau, answers numerous questions concerning U.S.
role in bringing peace between blacks and whites
without conflict.

454. Clough, Michael. "Beyond Constructive
      Engagement." Foreign Pol 61 (Winter
      1985/1986): 3-24.

        Clough states that Reagan's strategy
regarding South Africa has not worked and that a
new foreign policy should be developed to help
bring an end to apartheid in that country.

455. Coker, Christopher. "Retreat into the Future:
      The United States, South Africa, and Human
      Rights, 1976-8." J Mod Afric Stud 18: 3
      (1980): 509-524.

        Coker criticizes the Carter Administration
for its failure to introduce an effective human
rights policy in South Africa for blacks and
whites.

456. _____. "The United States and South Africa: Can
      Constructive Engagement Succeed?" Millennium
      11 (Autumn 1982): 223-241.

        Coker contends that "only by working with
the regime, not against it, could the United
States expect to influence South Africa's system
of apartheid."

457. Conrad, Thomas.   "South Africa Circumvents
        Embargo." Bull Atom Sci 42 (March 1986): 8-
        13.

        Conrad contends that the U.S. seeks to impose
     an embargo on Libya, but rules out sanctions
     against South Africa for her position on
     apartheid.

458. Conway, Robert.   "South Africa: Can U.S. Policies
        Influence Change?" Worldview 27 (January
        1984): 12-14.

        Conway contends that in order for U.S.
     policies to play a major role in bringing about a
     change in South Africa, there must be a change in
     incorrect thinking of the U.S.

459. Coxon, I.   "Burning Issue Which Has Blazed a
        Trail." Times Higher Educ Suppl no. 681
        (November 22, 1985): 12.

        Coxon observes the role of the British
     student's continuing struggle to bring an end to
     the system of apartheid.

460. Craig, Warren.   "The Divestiture Debate." New
        Jersey Rep 15 (july 1985): 6-13.

        Studies a bill passed in the New Jersey
     Assembly that would force the state to divest
     millions of dollars in pension funds from U.S.
     corporations that have investments in South
     Africa.

461. Crocker, Chester A.   "South Africa: Strategy for
        Change." For Affairs 59 (Winter 1980-91):
        323-351.

        Crocker feels that a policy of constructive
     engagement and not sanctions should be the
     approach that the U.S. and other western countries
     should use to approach South Africa if they hope
     to bring about a peaceful change.

462. _____. "A U.S. Policy for the '80's." Africa Rep 26 (January, February 1981): 7-14.

Crocker contends that "We need a stronger basis for approaching the question on nonviolent change within South Africa. The question, therefore, is what useful role we can play to help South Africans of all groups think their way from today's situation toward a nonracial future."

463. _____. "U.S. Response to Apartheid in South Africa." Dept State Bul 85 (June 1985): 38-40.

Crocker defends the current U.S. policy toward South Africa and feels that imposing new sanctions against that country would be headed in the wrong direction.

464. Curtis, Michael. "Africa, Israel, and the Middle East." Middle East R 17 (Summer 1985): 5-22.

The author focuses on the relationships between South Africa and Israel, Africa and the Arab countries, and the current apartheid crisis.

465. Dale, Richard. "South Africa and Namibia: Changing the Guard and Guarded Change." Curr Hist 76 (March 1979): 101-4+.

Dale explains the situation in South Africa in regard to other countries in Africa.

466. Danaher, Kevin. "Sanctions Against South Africa: Strategy for the Anti-Apartheid Movement in the 1980's." Ufahamu 10 (Fall/Winter 1980): 5-18.

467. _____. "South Africa, U.S. Policy and the Anti-Apartheid Movement." R Radical Pol Econ 11: 3 (1979): 42-59.

468. _____. "The U.S. and South Africa: Building the Base for Sanctions." Freedom Ways 21 (1981): 29-40.

Danaher seeks to present evidence on how and
why the United States has in the past and
continues to avoid imposing sanctions against
South Africa.

469. _____. "U.S. Policy Options Toward South Africa:
A Bibliographic Essay." Curr Bib African
Affairs 13, No. 1 (1980-81): 2-25.

470. Davies, Jennifer. "Economic Disengagement and
South Africa: The Effectiveness and
Feasibility of Implementing Sanctions and
Divestments." Law and Pol Int Bus 15 (1983):
529-563.

471. Davies, John. "U.S. Foreign Policy and the
Education of Black South Africans." Comp
Educ R 29 (May 1985): 171-188.

472. "Dealing with Apartheid." Newsweek 105 (March 11,
1985): 28-36+.

The article examines the things that
Americans are doing to bring an end to the system
of apartheid in South Africa.

473. Derven, Ronald. "Henry Parker Fights Apartheid
with Investment Clout: Connecticut's
Activist Treasurer Says Social Investing and
Making Money Are Not Mutually Exclusive
Objectives." Pension World 21 (August 1985):
37-39.

Observes Parker's stance on using pension
funds to invest in South Africa stocks for profit.

474. Dewart, Tracy. "The World Demands Sanctions: A
Chronology." So Africa 16: 2 (March 1983):
13, 16.

475. "The Divestment Dilemma: As More States and Localities Decide to Withdraw Public Funds from Investment in Firms Doing Business in South Africa, Pension Fund Administrators and Other Finance Officials Face Thorny Questions as They Implement Divestment Policies." <u>Govt Fin R</u> 2 (October 1986): 7-11.

476. "Divestments by 42 Institutions of Higher Education." <u>Chron Higher Educ</u> 30 (May 22, 1985): 16.

This article gives a list of U.S. institutions and student organizations that have decided to partially and fully divest their investments in companies doing business in South Africa.

477. Dore, Isaak I. "United Nations' Measures to Combat Racial Discrimination: Progress and Problems in Retrospect." <u>Denver J Int L and Pol</u> 10 (Winter 1981): 299-330.

478. Downey, Thomas J. "Reagan's Real Aims in South Africa." <u>Nation</u> 242 (February 8, 1986): 138-140.

Discusses the foreign policy of the Reagan Administration toward the southern African region. Also, the author takes a closer look at Reagan's policy of "constructive engagement."

479. Doyle, Mark. "Sanctions Against Apartheid: A Forgotten Strategy?" <u>West Africa</u> no. 3475 (March 19, 1984): 605-606.

Doyle examines Reginald Green's proposal for an all-out naval blockade of South Africa.

480. Draper, Joan. "West Vetoes Sanctions Vote." <u>South Africa</u> 14: 3 (May, June 1981): 6.

481. Dugard, John. "Silence Is Not Golden." <u>Foreign Pol</u> (Spring 1982): 37-48.

Dugard contends that the policy of the Reagan Administration is being viewed as in support of the policies of the South African government.

482. "Economic Sanctions Against South Africa." W Comp Pres Docs 21 (September 16, 1985): 1048-1051.

Reagan makes remarks concerning the signing of Executive Order 12532 and answers questions concerning the impact of these sanctions on the government of South Africa.

483. Egedo, Ihebom. "Nigeria and Apartheid: Her Position in the Commonwealth." Round Table (January 1987): 33-39.

Egedo reveals the government of Nigeria's views on apartheid and the Prime Minister's opposition to sanctions against South Africa.

484. Eickhoff, Ekkehard. "Aspects of German-South African Relations." Intl Affairs Bull 7: 1 (1983) 25-34.

In this address, Eickhoff mentions some of the differences and similarities of Germany and the South in regard to race relations.

485. "Ending Apartheid in South Africa." Dept State Bul 86 (September 1986): 1-17.

In an address before members of the World Affairs Council, Reagan gives his reasons for not imposing punitive sanctions against South Africa.

486. Evans, G. "College Students Show New Interest in Protesting Apartheid in South Africa." Chron Higher Educ 29 (February 6, 1985): 11-18.

Evans claims that the arrests of protesters in front of the South African embassy in Washington have increased U.S. college student's participation in the anti-apartheid movement.

487. F., M. "Apartheid, Getting by with a Little Help
     from Its Friends." So Africa 16: 2 (March
     1983): 10-12.

488. _____. "Legislators, Activists Meet." So Africa
     14: 4 (July-August 1981): 14-15, 31.

489. "Falling Short: Reaction to R. Reagan's Speech on
     South Africa." Time 128 (August 4, 1986):
     12-16+.

     This article reflects on the statements made
     by the President regarding sanctions against South
     Africa to bring an end to apartheid. It states
     that there are no major changes in the U.S. policy
     toward South Africa.

490. Farrell, C.S. "Anti-Apartheid Conference Votes to
     Blacklist Coaches Who Recruit South African
     Athletes." Chron Higher Educ 30 (May 29,
     1985): 27-28.

     Farrell claims that forty countries have
     voted to blacklist U.S. college coaches who
     recruit athletes in South Africa.

491. Feldmann, G. W. "South Africa: An International
     Issue." Africa Insight 12:2 (1982): 75-77,
     111.

     The author contends that the dispute between
     the white government of South Africa and the
     blacks should be settled through international
     supervision because it is an international
     problem.

492. Felton, John. "Administration's Role: How Much Is
     Enough?" Critics Say South Africans Get
     Mixed Signals." Cong Q W Rep 44 (June 21,
     1986): 1386-1387.

     Felton discusses the possibility of Congress
     imposing stiffer sanctions on the government of
     South Africa.

493. _____. "Bucking Strong Hill Sentiment, Reagan
          Vetoes South Africa Bill." Cong Q W Rep 44
          (September 27, 1986): 2268-2271.

     Felton covers information on U.S. policies in
     South Africa and the various sanctions levied by
     the U.S., Great Britain, and Japan.

494. _____. "Capitol Hill Taking a New Look at
          Apartheid." Cong Q W Rep 43 (March 9, 1985):
          440-448.

     Discusses the differences among the members
     of Congress as to what should be done by the U.S.
     to help bring an end to institutionalized racism
     in South Africa.

495. _____. "Conservatives in Congress Join in
          Campaign Against Apartheid: South Africa
          Warned of Sanctions." Cong Q W Rep 42
          (December 8, 1984): 3072-3073.

496. _____. "Hill Overides Veto of South Africa
          Sanctions." Cong Q W Rep 44 (October 4,
          1986): 2338-42.

496a. _____. "Pressure Builds for New South Africa
          Sanctions." Cong Q W Rep 44 (July 26, 1986):
          1671-1674.

     Felton relates that Congress is considering
     calling for a total trade embargo and requiring
     all U.S. firms to pull out of South Africa.

497. _____. "Reagan Averts a Confrontation on South
          Africa." Cong Q W Rep 43 (September 14,
          1985): 1800-1804.

     Felton contends that there are still a great
     deal of critics on Capitol Hill that are not
     pleased with Reagan's new stance on the fight
     against apartheid.

498. _____. "Troubled Future in Senate: Ways and Means
      Backs Apartheid Sanctions Bill." <u>Conq QW Rep</u>
      46 (July 30, 1988): 2087.

499. Fierce, Milfred C. "Black and White American
      Opinions Towards South Africa." <u>J Mod Afric
      Stud</u> 20: 4 (December 1982): 669-687.

      The author analyzes various opinion polls
      conducted on Americans' attitudes toward South
      Africa. She also takes a closer look at the way
      black Americans perceive the system of apartheid.

500. "Fighting Apartheid." <u>Common Cause Mag</u> 11 (May -
      June 1985): 33-37.

      Proponents and opponents debate whether
      economic sanctions are the best way to fight or
      dismantle apartheid.

501. Finnigan, William. "Coming Apart over Apartheid:
      The Story Behind the Republicans' Split on
      South Africa." <u>Mother Jones</u> 11 (April/May
      1986): 19-34.

502. Fisher, Marc. "Showdown over South Africa."
      <u>Change</u> 11 (February 1979): 26-30.

      Fisher examines the spread of student unrest
      on U.S. college campuses regarding universities'
      investments in South Africa.

503. "The Force of Protest." <u>Afr News</u> 15: 8 (August
      25, 1980): 5-6, 8-11.

      This article examines the various
      disinvestment groups and their constant struggle
      to keep this movement alive.

504. "Forum: The United States and South Africa."
      <u>Orbis</u> 31 (Spring 1987): 3-31.

This article contains such writings as, "Eliminate Apartheid" by Leon Sullivan; "The Case Against Disinvestment" by Per Duigan; "The U.S. Government Position", by J. Douglas Holladay, and "A New Policy -- Selective Engagement", by Henry Bienen.

505. Frank, Thomas M.   "On Investment and Boycott by the Developing Countries Against South Africa: A Rationale and Preliminary Assessment of Feasibility." Human Rights Q 4 (Summer 1982): 309-332.

506. Freeman, Linda.   "Canada and Africa in the 1970's." Intl Jnl 35: 4 (Autumn 1980): 794-820.

The author contends that Canada is not making any major changes in its policy toward the government of South Africa.

507. "The Future of the Commonwealth: Interview with Malcolm Fraser, 7 August 1986." Round Table (October 1986): 324-329.

Looks at the decision made at a summit to impose sanctions on the government of South Africa.

508. Gelb, Norman.   "Thatcher Takes on the Commonwealth: Staving Off Sanctions." New Leader 69 (July 14/28, 1986): 6-7.

Gelb talks about the disunity among members of the Commonwealth over Great Britain's reluctance to impose full sanctions against South Africa.

509. Omitted.

510. Gitlin, Todd.   "Divestment Stirs a New Generation." Nation 240 (May 18, 1985): 585-587.

The author touches upon the correlations
between university investments and apartheid in
South Africa.

511. Goell, Yosef. "Israel/South Africa: A View from
     Jerusalem." Africa Rep 25: 6 (November -
     December 1980): 18-22.

     Goell discusses the dilemma which Israel
faces by being allied with South Africa in view of
that country's racist policies.

512. Goldfield, Steve. "South Africa: The Israel
     Connection." Am - Arab Affairs (Fall 1986):
     106-129.

     Goldfield makes a comparison between
apartheid and Zionism and alludes to military and
trade cooperation between the countries.

513. Graves, Florence. "Spotlight on South Africa:
     South African Ambassador to the U.S.
     Bernardus Fourie Talks About His Government's
     Apartheid Policies." Common Cause Mag 11
     (May/June 1985): 28-32.

     Graves discusses the remarks made by Fourie
defending his country's policy of apartheid and
the proposed economic sanctions being considered
by the U.S.

514. Gray, William H., III. "Standing for Sanctions."
     Africa Rep 31 (March-April 1986): 27.

     The Congressman tells of his recent visit to
South Africa and his strong feelings about
economic sanctions on that country as a way of
bringing an end to apartheid.

515. Greene, E. "Campus Activities Expand Anti-
     Apartheid Drive, Seeking Aid for South
     African Liberation Groups." Chron Higher
     Educ 31 (November 27, 1985): 25-26.

Greene contends that students in the U.S. are
examining other methods of expanding the anti-
apartheid movement besides calling for
institutions to divest.

516. H., W. "The People Demand Sanctions." Africa 16:
     2 (March 1983): 19-22.

517. Haglund, David G. "South Africa, Minerals and
         Sanctions." Intl Perspect (May - June 1985):
         3-5.

     Covers different ways of how the U.S. can
reduce its dependence on minerals from South
Africa.

518. Hamilton, W.G. "Western European TNC's in South
         Africa." CTC Reporter (Spring 1987): 40-42.

     Hamilton talks about the role of the Sullivan
Principles and how Europe perceives the system of
apartheid.

519. Harris, Vincent. "Divestment Hits Apartheid in
         the Pocketbook." Black Sch 16
         (November/December 1985): 12-17.

     Harris reveals a campaign that seeks to force
the withdrawal of funds controlled by
institutional investors from U.S. financial
institutions and businesses that do business with
South Africa.

520. Hartley, William. "Behind South Africa's Turn
         Away from U.S." U S News World Rep (30 April
         1979): 32.

     Hartley feels that the relationship between
the U.S. and South Africa is about to fall apart
because Botha feels that the Carter Administration
is seeking to back the black rebels of South
Africa.

521. Hauser, Rita E. "Israel, South Africa and the
West." South Africa Intl 11: 2 (October
1980): 81-90.

The author analyzes the relationship between
Israel and South Africa and how the Carter
Administration directed its foreign policy toward
these two country.

522. Hayden, Bill. "Apartheid and South Africa." Aus
For Affairs Rec 56 (September 1985): 826-833.

Hayden says, "The Australian government
intends to play its part in getting the reform
process under way. It intends to do this through
its own forms of pressure on South Africa, through
its direct contacts with South Africa, through
CHOGM and the Commonwealth and through the UN."

523. Herbstein, Denis. "European Community: Under
Thatcher's Coattails." Africa Rep 31
(September/October 1986): 20-23.

The author talks about the members of the
economic European community and the measures they
are using against South Africa.

524. Hexter, Holly. "Conscientious Objectives:
Campuses Respond to South Africa." Educ Rec
66 (Fall 1985): 38-43.

Hexter believes that the activities being
undertaken by U.S. colleges and universities could
prove to be the most helpful contribution to
improving the quality of life for blacks in South
Africa.

525. Howard, William. "Lobbying Against Apartheid."
Africa Rep 33 (March/April 1988): 40-41.

526. Hudson, Darril. "The World Council of Churches
     and Racism in Southern Africa." Intl J 34: 3
     (1979) 475-500.

     Hudson outlines the objectives and activities
     of the World Council of Churches (WCC) in Southern
     Africa in regards to its care for victims of
     racism.

527. Hutchinson, John. "Reagan and South Africa: The
     Case for Urgent Understanding." Nat R 37
     (November 1, 1985): 25-26+.

     Hutchinson thinks that South Africa is
     looking to the U.S. for a solution to the racial
     problems in their country.

528. "Interview: Congressman William H. Gray, III."
     Africa Rep 30 (May/June 1985): 49-53.

     Gray explains why he advocates the Anti-
     Apartheid Act and gives his view of the potential
     impact of American sanctions against South Africa.

529. "Italy and the United Nations Faced with
     Apartheid: Italy's Contribution in the
     International Community Against Apartheid."
     Italy Docs and Notes 27 (March/April 1979):
     123-172.

530. Ivens, Michael. "The Corporate Role in Fighting
     Apartheid: British Style." Bus & Soc R
     (Summer 1986): 49-52.

     Ivens examines the assistance of British
     firms in South Africa and their push to bring
     about its economic development for blacks.

531. Jacob, Miriam. "Black Reactions to Reagan."
     Africa Rep 27 (July-August 1982): 48-51.

Jacob talks about the discontent of South
Africa's blacks with the Reagan Administration's
silence and institution of tougher reforms and
sanctions against the South African government.

532. Jackson, Jesse L. "Don't Adjust to Apartheid."
     Black Sch 15 (November/December 1984): 39-43.

Rev. Jackson criticizes the Reagan
Administration's policy of constructive
engagement. He contends that it is a policy
designed to let apartheid stay in place for quite
some time in South Africa.

533. Jankowitsch, Odette, and Seidensticker, Ellen.
     "Transnational Corporations in South Africa."
     Dissent 26 (Fall 1979): 473-77.

The authors examine the question concerning
corporations and their stand on apartheid and ask
are there any alternatives that can be implemented
without disrupting the economy of the country.

534. Jenkins, Simon. "America and South Africa: Anti-
     Apartheid Without Tears." Economist 294
     (March 30, 1985): 17-22+.

The author examines some of the strengths and
weaknesses of Reagan's policy of constructive
engagement.

535. Jerry, R.H. "U.S. Colleges and the Response to
     Apartheid [College Divestitute]." Chron
     Higher Educ 30 (April 3, 1985): 88.

Jerry believes that total divestiture from
all business in South Africa is not the best means
to end apartheid.

536. Kaempfer, William H. "Divestment, Investment,
     Sanctions, and Disinvestment: An Evaluation
     of Anti-Apartheid Policy Instruments." Int
     Org 41 (Summer 1987): 457-473.

537. Kalley, Jacqueline A. "Sanctions and Southern
     Africa: A Bibliographic Guide." Current Bib
     African Aff 14 (1981-1982): 201-234.

538. Kapstein, Jonathan. "Leaving South Africa." Bus
     Week (September 23, 1985): 104-107+.

     This article examines the problems that
corporations in South Africa are encountering and
why they are being forced to leave the country.

539. Katjavivi, Peter. "Why Sanctions Must Hit South
     Africa." New A (April 1981): 50-51.

540. Katzen, Leo. "South Africa's Vulnerability to
     Economic Sanctions." R Intl Stud 8: 2 (April
     1982): 89-98.

541. Kennedy, Edward M. "A Call For Justice: Senator
     Edward Kennedy's Recent Visit to South Africa
     Has Convinced Him of the Need for the U.S.
     Government to Play a More Active and Vocal
     Role in Opposing Apartheid." Africa Rep 30
     (May/June 1985): 10-13.

     The Senator mentions some of the aspects of
the proposed Anti-Apartheid Act of 1985.

542. _____. "The Sanctions Debate." Africa Rep 31
     (September/October 1986): 37-39.

     Kennedy testifies before the Senate Committee
concerning the reasons why he feels that sanctions
are the only means left to end the system of
apartheid.

543. Kennelly, Joe. "Apartheid Leads to Mass
     Unemployment." Afr Communist (1979): 31-46.

544. Kessler, Felix. "Goodyear Toughs It Out."
     Fortune 112 (September 30, 1985): 24-26.

Kessler examines Goodyear Tire and Rubber
Company's reasons for remaining in South Africa.

545. Kinnock, Neil. "South Africa: Measures That
     Matter." Round Table (January 1987): 22-32.

     The author shares his views of why he
     believes that imposing economic sanctions against
     South Africa will hasten the end of apartheid.

546. Knowles, Louis L. "Helping Apartheid Out." Found
     News, 26 (November-December 1985): 35-43.

     Knowles talks about the different types of
     economic sanctions being levied against South
     Africa.

547. Koenderman, Tony. "Sanctions." South Africa Intl
     9:3 (January 1979): 150-158.

548. Kohler, Volkmar. "The Problems in Southern Africa
     - A Challenge to European Policy." Afrika
     23: 12 (1982): 3-5.

548a. Kondracke, Morton. "Pry Freedom: Bush and
      Dukakis on Apartheid." New Repub 199 (July
      11, 1988): 16-18.

549. Kromer, R. "Constructive Engagement Pays - For
     Some." Chr & Crisis 45 (February 4 and 18,
     1985): 30-35.

     Kromer contends that there are quite a few
     people in Congress who are against the sale of
     supplies to South Africa that would bolster their
     military.

550. Kunnert, Dirk Thomas. "The South African Council
     of Churches and Disinvestment." J Contem
     Hist 15: 2 (December 1980): 1-33.

551. LaGuma, Alex. "Apartheid Is Not Just a Regional
     Problem." New W R 48 (March/April 1980): 18-
     21.

552. Lake, Anthony. "U.S. Policy Toward South Africa."
     Dept State Bul 79 (January 1979): 18-20.

     In this article, Lake claims that the U.S.
     hopes to promote constructive and peaceful changes
     in South Africa and bring an end to the practice
     of apartheid.

553. Leonard, Richard. "Business and South Africa:
     Pressures Against Apartheid Mount in the USA
     (Actions in the Congress and in State
     Legislatures and City Governments to Divest
     Holdings in Corporations and Banks Doing
     Business with South Africa)." Multi Bus
     (1984): 14-22.

554. Lovassy, Tamas. "International Efforts Towards
     the Prohibition of Apartheid." Dev and Peace
     1 (Autumn 1981): 200-218.

555. Lugar, Richard G. "Making Foreign Policy: The
     Congress and Apartheid; The Chairman of the
     Senate Foreign Relations Committee Discusses
     What Has Caused American Legislators to Alter
     the Course of U.S. Policy Toward Pretoria."
     Africa Rep 31 (September/October 1986): 33-
     36.

556. "Lutherans Move Against Apartheid." So Africa 15:
     4 (November 1982): 14.

     The Lutheran Church in America passes a
     resolution calling for economic and diplomatic
     sanctions against South Africa.

557. Lyman, Princeton. "U.S. Export Policy Toward
     South Africa." Dept State Bul 83 (May 1983):
     25-29.

     Lyman, Deputy Assistant Secretary for African
     Affairs, testifies before the subcommittee on
     Africa concerning the administration's policy of
     constructive engagement.

558. M., A. "Apartheid: A Crime Against Humanity." <u>So Africa</u>, 16: 2 (March 1983): 8-9.

Focuses on South Africa's attacks against neighboring countries and its illegal occupation of Namibia. Also, details are given of the oppression that is used by the government of South Africa through the system of apartheid, and there is a call for sanctions against the government in order to combat these human rights violations.

559. M., F. "Apartheid: Getting by with a Little Help from Its Friends." <u>So Africa</u> 16: 2 (March 1983): 10-12.

Contends that the U.S. and other western countries fail to enforce sanctions against South Africa because of their economic and political interest in that region.

559a. Mackenzie, Hilary. "The Ranks on Apartheid: Commonwealth Foreign Ministers Unable to Agree on New Sanctions Against South Africa." <u>Macl Mag</u> 101 (August 15, 1988): 13.

560. Maddrey, Wendell C. "Economic Sanctions Against South Africa: Problems and Prospects for Enforcement of Human Rights Norms." <u>Va J Intl L</u> 22 (Winter 1982): 345-380.

561. Madison, Christopher. "South African Embassy Has a Tough Job Trying to Ward Off Economic Sanctions." <u>Natl J</u> 17 (February 16, 1985): 371-373.

Discusses South Africa's efforts to persuade Congress not to impose economic sanctions against their country.

562. Maitama-Jule and Alhaji Yusuff. "Africa, the United States and South Africa." <u>Africa Rep</u> 27:5 (September-October 1982): 10-13.

The ambassador contends "that sanctions are the only nonviolent means of ending apartheid."

563. Malan, Theo. "South Africa and Economic
          Sanctions." South Africa Found News 7: 2
          (February 1981): 2-3.

564. Manning, Robert A. "Toward Constructive
          Disengagement?" Africa Rep 30 (September-
          October 1985): 82-85.

     Contends that Reagan's policy is becoming
weak due to events taking place in South Africa
and activities happening in the U.S. Congress.

565. Mashen, G. "Australians Enforce Sanctions."
          Times Higher Educ Supp no. 666 (August 9,
          1985):9.

     The author reveals that institutions of
higher learning in Australia have begun to
institute bans on any dealings with South Africa.
This was due in part to the government's support
of France's United Nations security council
resolution calling for a ban on future investments
in South Africa.

566. Massing, Michael. "South Africa: The Business of
          Fighting Apartheid." Atl Mo 259 (February
          1987): 26-32.

     The author contends that U.S. companies,
whether they decide to stay or leave, have very
little impact on apartheid.

567. Mathews, J. "South Africa's External Economic
          Relations." J Wld Trade Law 13, No. 6
          (November/December 1979): 495-509.

     The author contends that "Due to the
relationships between South Africa and other
countries, there is no doubt that economic
sanctions would affect not only her local
population and neighbors, but also many trading
partners, who would lose a valuable market for
industrial products."

568. McQuaid, E.P. "South African Protest Goes into
        Second Year." <u>Times High Educ Suppl</u> no. 599
        (April 27, 1984): 9.

        The author observes the strategy of the
    students at Harvard University in their ongoing
    struggle to try and convince that university to
    divest all of its stocks associated with South
    Africa.

569. Mehlman, Maxwell J. "United States Restrictions
        on Exports to South Africa." <u>Am J Intl Law</u>
        73(October 1979): 581-603.

        This article examines the history of U.S.
    restrictions of exports to South Africa and gives
    recommendations that would bring about a more
    effective change in dismantling the policy of
    apartheid.

570. Metz, Steven Kent. "The Anti-Apartheid Movement
        and the Formulation of American Policy Toward
        South Africa, 1969-1981." The Johns Hopkins
        University, <u>DAI</u>, 1985, 46: 2066-A.

        Metz feels that the movement in the U.S.
    failed to persuade the U.S. government to take a
    more active stance against the government of South
    Africa and its policy of apartheid.

571. Miller, Frederic A., and Arnold, Bob. "The Screws
        Are Tightening on U.S. Companies." <u>Bus Week</u>
        (February 11, 1985): 38-40.

        This article contends that U.S. businesses
    are feeling pressure at home and abroad to stop
    doing business with South Africa.

572. Minter, William. "South Africa: Straight Talk on
        Sanctions." <u>Foreign Pol</u> no. 65 (Winter 1986-
        87): 43-63.

Minter discusses the recent economic sanctions imposed against South Africa by the U.S. and the effects they will have in South Africa.

573. Morrell, Louis R. "Making the Right Investment Decisions." AGB Rept 26 (July-August 1984): 16-19.

574. "Multi-Part Resolution on South Africa Apartheid." UN Chron 20 (February 1983): 34-36.

The U.N. General Assembly lists a number of resolutions passed regarding the dismantling of apartheid.

575. Murray, Roger. "Who Trades with South Africa?" Afr Bus No. 12 (August 1979): 11-12.

576. Myers, Desaix, III, and David M. Liff. "The Press of Business: South Africa Under Botha." Foreign Pol (Spring 1980): 143-63.

The authors contend that it would take U.S. business along with the U.S. government to continue pressure on South Africa that would lead to a change in that country's racial problems.

577. _____. "South Africa Under Botha (2): The Press of Business." Foreign Pol (Spring 1980): 143-163.

Contends that as long as American companies continue to do business in South Africa, they can put themselves in position to influence certain changes in that country.

578. Ndaba, David. "Sanctions and the Struggle: An Interview with... by James Khatomi." So Africa 16: 2 (March 1983): 23-24.

Ndaba talks about the ANC's campaign to isolate and weaken the government of South Africa.

578a. Nemeth, Mary. "Canada in a Hot Seat: Business
       Transactions with South Africa Questioned."
       Macl Mag 102 (February 20, 1989): 21.

579. Nielson, John. "Time to Quit South Africa."
       Fortune 112 (September 30, 1985): 18-23.

       This article examines those U.S. companies
       that have left the country and looks at those that
       remain despite political and economic pressure.

580. Nnadili, Anthony O. "Decision-Making in the
       United Nations Security Council: A Case Study
       of the Race Conflict in South Africa
       Resulting from the Policies of Apartheid."
       Howard University, DAI, 1984, 46: 1035-A.

       The author attempts to explain the weaknesses
       of the U.S. Security Council regarding sanctions
       against South Africa for its racial policies.

581. North, James. "Divestment Imperative." New Repub
       192 (March 25, 1985): 10-12.

       North states, "Americans of all political
       persuasions are starting to realize that there is
       a terrifying sense of urgency about South Africa's
       slide toward the edge."

582. "Notes and Comments: Differences between Current
       Anti-Apartheid Protests and the Protests of
       the 1960's." NY 61 (May 6, 1985): 35-36.

583. Olson, Martha J. "University Investments with a
       South African Connection: Is Prudent
       Divestiture Possible?" NY Univ J Intl Law
       Pol 11:3 (1979): 543-580.

584. Ottaway, David. "Africa: U.S. Policy Eclipse."
       For Affairs 58 (No. 3, 1980): 637-658.

       Ottaway contends that black Africans view the
       U.S. policy as one that looks at the African
       countries as no more than pawns in the cold war.

585. Parsons, A. R. "World Conference on Sanctions
     Against South Africa: Australian Statements."
     Aus For Affairs Rec 57 (June 1986): 477-479.

586. Pehe, Jiri. "South Africa Through East European
     Eyes." Free at Issue (March/April, 1986):
     13-14.

     Pehe makes a comparison between the policies
     of apartheid and those of other authoritarian
     governments. Also, he looks at the possibility of
     gradual reform of those policies in South Africa.

586a. Poewe-Hexham, Karla O. "Charismatic Churches and
     the Struggle Against Apartheid: A Dispute."
     Chr Cent 106 (January 4-11, 1989): 16+.

587. Pohl, Keith I. "The Ethics of Disinvestment."
     Chr Cent 102 (August 28-September 4, 1985):
     759-760.

     Pohl contends that "It is better ethically
     to push all influential American business into
     higher social responsibility than it is to flee
     the scene and hope to create a changed society out
     of the imagined economic vacuum."

588. "The Policy of American Universities Towards
     Divestment in South Africa." Minerva 24
     (Summer/Autumn/1986): 246-343.

     Covers policy statements of 10 universities
     in regard to divestment. Also it lists a table of
     112 colleges and universities that have divested
     as of May 1986.

588a. Pressman, Steven. "Apartheid Foes Look to New
     Sanctions in 1988: Frustration With Reagan
     Policy in South Africa." Cong Q W Rep 45
     (November 14, 1987): 2792-2793.

589. "Protestors Target Economic Ties." Afr News 14:
     (April 1980): 7-10.

        Examines the attitude of Americans regarding
investments in South Africa as a way to express
dismay about the practice of apartheid in that
country. Also, it looks at the various groups in
the U.S. that are responsible for disinvestments
in South Africa.

590. Raiford, William. "South Africa: Foreign
        Investment and Separate Development." Issue
        9: 1,2 (Spring, Summer 1979): 30-36.

        The author examines the system of apartheid
and the U.S. policy toward this system and it
hopes to evoke peaceful change in that country.

591. Ray, J.J. "Present and Future Changes in South
        Africa: A Comment on Vale." Contemp R 247
        (August 1985): 82-85.

        Ray talks about his disagreement with Cdm.
Vale's statement that change in the current status
of blacks and whites in South Africa will not
work.

592. Reagan, Ronald. "Economic Sanctions Against South
        Africa: Executive Order 12-522." W Comp Pres
        Docs 21 (September 16, 1985): 1051-1054.

        The President details some of the sanctions
that are being placed against South Africa in an
effort to end that country's system of apartheid.

593. _____. "U.S. Economic Relations with South
        Africa." Vital Speeches 52 (August 15,
        1986): 642-645.

        Reagan talks about dismantling the system of
apartheid but disagrees with economic sanctions as
a means of achieving this goal.

594. _____. "World Affairs Council and the Foreign
        Policy Association: Remarks to Members, July
        22, 1986." W Comp Pres Docs 22 (July 28,
        1986): 975-980.

Reagan alludes to the U.S. policy toward
South Africa.

595. Reddy, Enuga S. "Decades of Resistance." _Africa
      Rep_ 30 (September/October 1985): 56-60.

Reddy looks at the system of apartheid and
how the United Nations has worked to bring an end
to this system.

596. Redekop, Clarence G. "The Mulroney Government and
      South Africa: Constructive Disengagement."
      Behind the Headlines 44 (December 1986): 16.

596a. Reed, David. "Do South African Sanctions Make
      Sense?" _Read Digest_ 134 (February 1989):
      51-56.

This article reveals that the Canadian
government could play an important role in
establishing a relationship with South Africa in
promoting better race relations within that
country.

597. Omitted.

598. St. Jorre, John de. "South Africa: Is Change
      Coming?" _For Affairs_ 60: 1 (Fall 1981): 106-
      122.

The author states that without a settlement
being made on Nambia the revamped U.S. policy
toward South Africa will be of little
significance.

599. Samuels, Michael A. "U.S.-South African Relations
      Now." _Free at Issue_ (July-August 1982): 16-
      19.

Samuels examines the Reagan administration
and what direction it will take in bringing about
a peaceful change in South Africa.

600. Saxena, S.C. "Apartheid: The Role of U.S. and
Multi-Nationals. Ins Def Stud J 21 (July-
September 1979): 43-57.

601. _____. "The Problem of Apartheid: Sinister Role
of U.S. Capital." Pol Service R 18: 2
(1979).

602. Schlegel, John P. "Twenty Years of Policy
Evolution: Canada, the U.S.A. and South
Africa." Round Table (January 1987): 40-52.

603. Schneider, William. "Public Has Doubts About
South Africa Sanctions." Natl J 17 (August
17, 1985): 1912-1913.

Schneider discusses the views of the U.S.
public about the usefulness of sanctions and
embargoes as   means of forcing policy change in
South Africa.

604. "The Screws Are Tightening on U.S. Companies."
Bus Week No. 2880 (February 11, 1985): 38-40.

Looks at the external pressures being placed
on American companies in South Africa to divest
all of their economic ties with South African
operations.

605. Seidman, Ann. "Why U.S. Corporations Should Get
Out of South Africa (In Terms of South
Africa's Race and Human Relations Policies
and Its Growing Military Industrial
Complex)." Issue 9 (Spring/Summer 1979): 37-
41.

606. Seiler, John. "South African Response to External
Pressure." Intl Affairs Bull 3: 1 (1979): 7-
14.

606a. Seligman, Daniel. "Feeling Good about South
          Africa: Divestment." _Fortune_ 117 (May 23,
          1988): 118.

607. Sethi, S. "How the United States Can Fight
        Apartheid." _Bus & Soc R_ (Summer 1986): 58-
        61.

        Sethi talks about the various policy options
     of economic sanctions and foreign aid for U.S.
     corporations in South Africa.

608. Shepard, Robert B. "South Africa: The Case for
        Disengagement." _Nat Interest_ no. 2 (Winter
        1986): 46-62.

        This article covers the debate in the U.S.
     between the Reagan administration and his critics
     regarding economic sanctions.

609. "Should the U.S. Impose Sanctions? (As a Means of
        Curbing South African Apartheid Policies;
        Seminar Proceedings)." _Trans Afr Forum_ 2
        (Fall 1983): 31-49.

610. Shultz, George D. "U.S./South Africa: Toward a
        New South Africa." _Africa Rep_ 31
        (September/October 1986): 16-19.

        Shultz calls for a peaceful change in South
     Africa, not the use of economic sanctions.

611. _____. "The U.S. Approach to South Africa." _Dept
        Stat Bul_ 86 (September 1986): 5-12.

        Shultz talks about the various aspects of the
     U.S. policy toward South Africa.

612. Sincere, Richard E. "The Politics of Sentiment:
        U.S. Churches Approach Investment in South
        Africa." _South Afr Intl_ 14:3 (January 1984):
        453-466.

613. _____. "The Churches and Investment in South
         Africa." America 150 (March 3, 1984): 145-
         149.

     Sincere studies the National Council of
     Churches involvement of responsible investment in
     South Africa.

614. Smiley, Xan. "A Black South Africa?" Economist
     298 (February 1, 1986): 33-40.

     The author examines the true meaning of
     apartheid for the bulk of South Africans and the
     world.

615. Smith, Lee. "South Africa: Time to Stay- or GO?"
     Fortune 114 (August 4, 1986): 46-48.

     Smith examines the pros and cons of
     whether it is better for U.S. companies to stay in
     South Africa and try to enforce change or leave
     due to the mounting criticism at home.

616. "South Africa and the International Community in
         the 1980's." Intl Affairs Bull 4: 1 (1980):
         3-42.

617. "South Africa in the World: Four Views." South
         Africa Int Q 14: 4 (April 1984): 502-519.

618. "South Africa: Is There a Peaceful Path to
         Pluralism? a Symposium." Bus & Soc R
         (Spring 1986): 4-128.

     The article details the views of several
     spokespersons of political and pressure groups
     from around the country. Also, it examines the
     role of U.S. foreign policy regarding sanctions
     against South Africa.

619. "South Africa Sanctions." Cong Q W Rep 45: 9
         (February 28, 1987): 370.

Senator Lugar questions the reasons behind
the Reagan administration's veto blocking
sanctions against South Africa by the United
Nations.

620. "South Africa: Sanctions and Beyond; Cover Story."
Africa No. 181 (September 1986): 8-12, 14.

Studies Great Britain's economic and trade
relations with South Africa.

621. "South Africa: Straight Talk on Sanctions."
Foreign Pol (Winter 1986/1987): 43-63.

Discusses the political and economic effects
of U.S. sanctions on South Africa.

622. "South Africa: The Hard Questions." America 153
(August 10, 1985): 45-63.

A group of experts examines the idea of
whether or not economic sanctions against South
Africa would help people whom it was intended to
help.

623. "South African Embassy Has a Tough Job Trying to
Ward Off Economic Sanctions: Congress Is
Weighing Legislation That Would Punish South
Africa for Its Policy of Apartheid, and That
Government Is Lobbying to Persuade Congress
Not to Act." Natl J 17 (February 16, 1985):
371-373.

624. "South African Sport: Apartheid's Achilles Heel?
(Whether Responses and Policies, Especially
by Western and Commonwealth Countries Are
Effective in Their Declared Objective of
Helping to End Apartheid; Efforts in South
Africa Towards Integrating Sports
Activities)." Wld Today 40 (June 1984): 234-
243.

625. "Southern Africa: A New Approach." Round Table
(July 1987): 322-332.

Studies the use of psychological and
political sanctions rather than economic sanctions
as   means to bring an end to apartheid.

626. "Special Issue on the Divestment Campaign in the
     U.S. Apartheid, and the Implications of
     Multinational Involvement in South Africa."
     Multinatl 6 (June 30, 1985): 1-7.

627. "Special Report: Sanctions." So Africa 16 (March
     1983): 7-26.

628. "Special Report: South Africa Sanctions." Cong Q
     W Rep 43 (March 9, 1985): 440-448.

     Outlines the various economic and political
sanctions imposed by Reagan on the government of
South Africa. These sanctions are a part of the
anti-apartheid bill (HR1460).

629. Spring, Beth. "Falwell Raises a Stir by Opposing
     Sanctions Against South Africa." Christ Tod
     29 (October 4, 1985): 52-54+.

     Spring states that many Christian leaders in
the U.S. oppose Falwell's ideology regarding the
system of apartheid in South Africa.

630. Stultz, Newell M. "Bridging the Black-White Gulf
     in Africa." Orbis 25 (Winter 1982): 881-902.

     Stultz discusses the Ford and Carter
administrations and their attempts to bring about
a more suitable political condition for blacks and
whites in South Africa.

631. _____. "Sanctions, Models of Change and South
     Africa." South Africa Intl 13: 2 (October 1982):
     121-129.

     Stultz presents his findings on a study he
did while in South Africa regarding the issue of
international sanctions as a means of eliminating
apartheid.

632. Sullivan, Leon. "Agents for Change: The
     Mobilization of Multinational Companies in
     South Africa." Law and Pol Int Bus 15, no.
     2: (1983): 427-444.

     Studies the use of the Sullivan Principles as
     a means of mobilizing American multinationals to
     oppose apartheid.

633. _____. "The Sullivan Principles and Change in
     South Africa." Africa Rep 29 (May/June
     1984): 48-50.

     Sullivan details the effectiveness of his
     proposed rules of behavior for U.S. companies in
     dismantling the system of apartheid.

634. Suzman, Helen. "What America Should Do About
     South Africa." NY Times M (August 3, 1986):
     14-17.

     A liberal member of South Africa Parliament
     explains why sanctions against her country would
     hurt blacks more than whites.

634a. Tambo, Oliver. "Strategic Options for
     International Companies: The South African
     Crisis." Black Sch 18 (November/December
     1987): 8-13.

635. "Text Calling for Sanctions Against South Africa
     Vetoed in Council." UN Chron 25 (June 1988):
     54-55.

635a. "Text of Reagan's Sanctions Announcement." Cong Q
     W Rep 43 (September 14, 1985): 1834-1836.

     Reagan outlines the various sanctions that
     were placed on South Africa and what he hopes to
     accomplish from these measures.

636. Toler, Deborah. "Constructive Engagement:
     Reactionary Pragmatism at Its Best." Issue
     12 (Fall-Winter 1982): 11-18.

637. "Trade Embargo Would Render South Africa's Economy
      Vulnerable." U N Mon Chron 18 (July 1981):
      40-49.

      The Organization of African Unity and
      international non-governmental organizations give
      their reasons for requesting mandatory economic
      sanctions against South Africa.

638. "Transnational Corporations in South Africa and
      Namibia." Intl Comm Jurist R (June 1986):
      34-38.

      This report summarizes the recommendations of
      a panel appointed by the U.N. which proposed
      conditions under which the corporations should
      divest.

639. Ungar, Sanford J., and Vale, Peter. "South
      Africa: Why Constructive Engagement Failed."
      For Affairs 64 (Winter 1985/1986): 234-258.

      The author feels that the economic sanctions
      imposed by Reagan will not help to bring about a
      meaningful change to the racist system in South
      Africa.

640. _____. "South Africa's Lobbyists." NY Times M
      (October 13, 1985): 30+.

      The article tells about South Africa's
      attempt to influence U.S. opinion.

641. "Urgent Appeals Made for Mandatory Sanctions
      Against South Africa: Assembly Adopts 13
      Texts on Apartheid, Namibia." UN Chron 25
      (March 1988): 61-63.

642. "U.S. Policy Toward South Africa: Pros and Cons."
      Cong Dig 64 (October 1985): 225-256.

      Examines the proposed Anti-Apartheid Act of
      1985.

643. Wall, Patrick. "Major Patrick Wall: British
      Conservative Member of Parliament." *Africa
      Rep* 25:5 (September-October 1980): 19-20.

      Wall expresses his views as to why he opposes
      sanctions against South Africa.

644. Walt, Vivienne. "Botswana: Feeling the Heat; by
      Virtue of Geographic Proximity, Botswana is
      Linked to the South African Economy and to
      the Increasing Violence Spilling over Its
      Borders; While Sanctions Against Pretoria Will
      Inevitably Affect Botswana Economy, President
      Quett Masire's Government Has Little Choice
      but to Support Their Implementation in Hopes
      of Bringing a Quicker End to Apartheid."
      Africa Rep 30 (November/December 1985): 64-
      67.

645. Walters, Ronald. "Beyond Sanctions: A
      Comprehensive U.S. Policy for Southern
      Africa." *Wld Pol J* 4 (Winter 1986/1987): 91-
      110.

      Walters feels that U.S. military and economic
      aid for South Africa's neighbors could help bring
      an end to apartheid.

646. Watson, Russell. "The Friends of Mr. Botha."
      Newsweek 106 (September 2, 1985): 30-32.

      Conservatives in America debate whether or
      not they should support sanctions imposed against
      South Africa by the U.S.

647. Whitaker, Mark. "What Can Be Done?" *Newsweek* 106
      (September 16, 1985): 16-22, 25-27, 30-33.

      The civil turmoil in South Africa has forced
      a change in the U.S. policy regarding sanctions.

647a. Whitehead, John C. "The Potential Impact of
      Imposing Sanctions Against South Africa."
      Dept. State Bul 88 (August 1988): 58-62.

648. Wiener, Jon. "Students, Stocks and Shanties."
     <u>Nation</u> 243 (October 11, 1986): 337-340.

     Wiener talks about the various campus
     divestment movements in the U.S. and what they
     have accomplished in bringing about an awareness
     of the racial system in South Africa.

649. Wilkins, Roger. "Africa in the U.S.:
     Demonstrating Our Opposition; Since Last
     November, The Free South Africa Movement Has
     Been in the Forefront of American Anti-
     Apartheid Activism." <u>Africa Rep</u> 30 (May/June
     1985): 29-32.

650. Willers, David. "The Disinvestment Debate."
     <u>Africa Rep</u> 27: 5 (September-October 1982):
     45-49.

     The author feels that the problem facing the
     Reagan Administration is how it could support U.S.
     corporations in South Africa and yet convince
     these companies to practice fair labor and promote
     racial change as well.

651. Williams, Franklin H. "South Africa Reforms and
     U.S. Foreign Policy." <u>USA Today</u> 113 (July
     1984): 32-35.

     The author states that the U.S. government is
     either not aware of or fails to realize that the
     reforms proposed by the South African government
     are not of any real significance in bringing about
     a change in that country.

652. Winkler, K.J. "Two Groups of Historians Vote to
     Divest Stocks as Protest Against Apartheid."
     <u>Chron Higher Educ</u> 30 (May 1, 1985): 1+.

     The member of the executive board of the
     Organization of American Historians passed a
     resolution requiring the association to sell its
     holdings in those companies doing business in
     South Africa.

653. Winston, Henry. "South Africa and the Reagan
          Factor." Polit Aff 65 (February 1986): 7-11.

     The author criticizes the U.S. foreign policy
toward South Africa's system of apartheid and
calls for overall sanctions against that country.

654. Woods, Donald. "Donald Woods: South African
          Opposition Journalist." Africa Rep 25: 5
          (September-October 1980): 21-22.

     Woods explains his reasons for asking for an
oil boycott against South Africa, and he feels
that it is the most effective means to bring an
end to apartheid.

655. Wright, Sanford. "Comprehensive International
          Sanctions Against South Africa: An Evaluation
          of Costs and Effectiveness." Afr Today 33
          (Second/Third Quarters 1986): 5-24.

     Wright examines the impact of the costs of
economic sanctions against the government of South
Africa and its neighbors.

656. _____. "Struggling Against Apartheid: The Use of
          Economic Sanctions on South Africa (Position
          of the United States in Relation to South
          Africa's Economy)." R Black Pol Econ 13
          (Winter 1984-1985): 37-47.

     Talks about the relationship between the U.S.
and South Africa and how the U.S. could help to
bring an end to the system of apartheid.

657. Zinn, Kenneth. "Americans Can Help End Apartheid:
          Disinvest Now!" Soc Sci Rec 22:2 (Fall
          1985): 12-14.

     Zinn claims that Americans can help bring an
end to the system of apartheid by disinvesting all
funds and monies associated with South Africa.

658. Zunes, Stephen. "Friends of Apartheid."
          Progressive (Fall 1979): 42-44.

Documents

659. Bok, Derek C. Reflecting on Divestment of Stock:
     An Open Letter to the Harvard Community.
     Washington, D.C.: Educational Resources
     Information Center, 1979. (ED 179 161).

     The President of Harvard discusses the
     possibility of his university selling its stock in
     U.S. companies doing business in South Africa, as
     a means to push for social and political change in
     that country.

660. Crocker, Chester A. South Africa: Report on the
     President's Executive Order. Washington,
     D.C.: G.P.O., 1986. (S1. 71/4-817).

661. _____. The U.S. Response to Apartheid in South
     Africa: April 17, 1985. Washington, D.C.:
     U.S. Dept. of State, 1985. (S1.71/4-688).

662. Robertson, William B. U.S. Wants an End to
     Apartheid. Washington, D.C.: U.S. Dept. of
     State, 1986.

663. Saxe, Joel. South Africa Divestiture Target
     Report No. 11. Washington, D.C.: Educational
     Resources Information Center, 1979. 21 pp.
     (ED172623).

     Saxe examines the student anti-apartheid
     movement and divestiture activities of U.S.
     students.

664. U.N. General Assembly. A/34/719. Policies of
     Apartheid of the Government of South Africa:
     Letter Dated 23 November, 1979 from the
     Permanent Representative of the Libyan-Arab
     Delegation to the United Nations Addressed to
     the Secretary-General on 23 November, 1979.
     3 pp.

665. _____. A/35/22. Report of the Special Committee
     Against Apartheid. 1980. 118 pp.

666. _____. A/40/22/Add.1. Special Report of the
     Special Committee Against Apartheid:
     Implementation of the Arms Embargo Against
     South Africa. 14 October 1985. 31 pp.

667. _____. A/40/22/Add. 3. Special Report of the
     Special Committee Against Apartheid: Further
     Action to Intensify Efforts to Inform World
     Public Opinion and Encourage Wider Public
     Action in Support of the Just Struggle of the
     Oppressed People of South Africa. 14 October
     1985. 13 pp.

668. _____. A/AC. 115/L. 509. Letter dated 28
     February 1979 addressed to the Chairman of
     the Special Committee against Apartheid from
     the Chairman of the South African Non-Racial
     Olympic Committee (San-Roc): issued in
     accordance with the decision taken by the
     Special Committee against Apartheid at its
     413th meeting held on 9 March 1979-30 March
     1979. 1 p.

669. _____. A/AC. 115/L. 520. Statement Made by Mr.
     Abdul S. Minty, Honorary Secretary of the
     British Anti-Apartheid Movement at the 448th
     Meeting of the Special Committee Held on
     Thursday, 6 March 1980-31 March 1980. 9 pp.

670. _____. A/AC. 115/L. 525. Declaration of the
     Hemispheric Seminar on Women Under Apartheid
     Held in Montreal, Canada, From 9 to 11 May
     1980. Issued in Accordance with the Decision
     Taken by the Special Committee against
     Apartheid at its 456th Meeting Held on 6 June
     1980-12 June 1980. 3 pp.

671. _____. A/AC. 115/L. 546. International Day for
     the Elimination of Racial Discrimination:
     Messsage Received by the Special Committee
     Against Apartheid (Issued in Accordance with
     the Decision Taken by the Special Committee
     at its 470th Meeting on 21 March 1980). 28
     April 1981. 54 pp.

672. _____. A/AC. 115/L. 566. Message from the United
      Nations to Special Committee Against
      Apartheid Addressed to H.E.M. Francois
      Mitterand, President of France, 24 March
      1982. 2 pp.

673. _____. A/Conf. 137/BP.4 South Africa: The Case
      for Mandatory Economic Sanctions. World
      Conference on Sanctions Against Racist South
      Africa. 15 May 1986. 21 pp.

674. _____. A/Conf. 137/Ref. 8. Bishop Desmond Tutu
      Calls upon the International Community to
      Apply Punitive Sanctions Against the
      Apartheid Regime. World Conference on
      Sanction Against Racist South Africa. 29
      April 1986. 6 pp.

675. _____. Plan of Action for the Promotion of the
      International Campaign Against Apartheid
      Secretariat. Department of Political and
      Security Council Affairs. Centre Against
      Apartheid. 1986. 17 pp.

676. _____. UNST/PSCA (05) N911. Analytical
      Compendium of Actions by Governments With
      Respect to Sanctions on South Africa. By
      Paul Conlon. Secretariat. Department of
      Political and Security Council Affairs.
      Centre Against Apartheid. September 1986. 20
      pp.

677. _____. UNST/PSCA (05)/N911. Calls for Concerted
      International Action Against Apartheid in
      South Africa. Secretariat. Department of
      Political and Security Council Affairs.
      Centre Against Apartheid. December 1985. 12
      pp.

678. _____. UNST/PSCA (05)/N911. Declaration of the
      International Seminar on the United Nations
      Arms Embargo Against South Africa.
      Secretariat. Department of Political and
      Security Council Affairs. Centre Against
      Apartheid. August 1986. 8 pp.

679. _____. UNST/PSCA (05)/N911. Special Committee
Against Apartheid and Anti-Apartheid
Movements Decide on Strategy to Intensify
International Campaign Against Apartheid.
Secretariat. Department of Political and
Security Council Affairs. Centre Against
Apartheid. December 1985. 43 pp.

680. _____. UNST/PSCA (05)N911. United States Student
Movement Against Apartheid: Hearings at
United Nations Headquarters on 27 June 1986
by the Secretariat. Department of Political
and Security Council Affairs. Centre Against
Apartheid. September 1986. 48 pp.

681. U.S. Congress House. Subcommittee on Africa.
Current Crisis in South Africa. 98th Cong.,
2nd Sess., December 4, 1984. Washington,
D.C.: Congressional Information Service, 20
pp. (H381-26).

Members of this subcommittee present
statements on the current U.S. policy toward South
African racial discrimination system.

682. _____. Subcommittee on Africa. Developments in
South Africa: U.S. Policy Responses. 99th
Cong., 2nd Sess., March 12, 1986.
Washington, D.C.: Congressional Information
Service, 126 pp. (H381-64).

683. _____. Subcommittee on Africa. Legislation Urging
the South African Government to Engage in
Meaningful Negotiations with That Country's
Black Majority. 99th Cong., 2nd Sess., June
24, 1986. Washington, D.C.: Congressional
Information Service, 68 pp. (H381-24).

684. _____. Subcommittee on Africa. South Africa
Legislation. 98th Cong., 2nd Sess., April 10,
1984. Washington, D.C.: Congressional
Information Service, 117 pp. (H381-22).

The subcommittee reviews several resolutions
relating to South Africa's racial policies.

685. _____. Subcommitte on Africa. <u>U.S. Policy Toward
      Southern Africa: Focus on Namibia, Angola,
      and South Africa</u>. 97th Cong., 1st Sess.,
      September 16, 1981. Washington, D.C.:
      Congressional Information Service, 61 pp.
      (H381-39).

      The members of this committee review the
      resolution that will not allow the South African
      Rugby Team to play in the U.S.

686. _____. Committee on Banking, Finance and Urban
      Affairs. <u>Anti-Apartheid Act of 1986</u>. 99th
      Cong., 2nd Sess., H.R. 4868. June 10, 1986.
      Washington, D.C.: G.P.O., 1986. 65 pp.
      (44.1322/1:99-81).

687. _____. Committee on Banking Finance and Urban
      Affairs. <u>Multilateral Development Bank
      Lending for Africa</u>. 99th Cong., 2nd Sess.,
      Washington, D.C.: G.P.O., 1986. 265 pp.

688. _____. <u>Impact of Withdrawal and Disinvestment from
      South Africa on the U.S. Economy</u>. 99th
      Cong., 1st Sess., Serial No. 99-40. September
      26, 1986. Washington, D.C.: Congressional
      Information Service, 268 pp. (H241-5).

      The Subcommittee on Domestic Monetary Policy
      examines the operations of U.S. corporations in
      South Africa and what steps should be taken to
      expedite withdrawal of these industries.

689. _____. <u>National Emergency with Respect to South
      Africa: Message from the President</u>. 99th
      Cong., 1st Sess., H. Doc. 99-103. September
      9, 1985. Washington, D.C.: Congressional
      Information Service, 4 pp. (H380-13).

      The President declares a national emergency
      and establishes sanctions against South Africa due
      to its continued posture on the system of
      apartheid.

690. _____. Subcommittee on Financial Institutions
     Supervision, Regulation, and Insurance. <u>South
     African Restrictions</u>. 98th Cong., 1st Sess.,
     Serial No. 98-32. June 8, 1983. Washington,
     D.C.: Congressional Information Service, 289
     pp. (H241-56).

     This subcommittee has decided to study H.R.
     1693 that establishes fair employment principles
     for U.S. firms operating in South Africa, and it
     would also prohibit U.S. bank loans to the South
     African Government.

691. _____. Committee on Foreign Affairs. <u>Calls for the
     Immediate Release of Detained Children Under
     Emergency Regulations in South Africa</u>. 100th
     Cong., 1st Sess., H.R. 141 and H.R. 214.
     July 29, 1987. Washington, D.C.: G.P.O.,
     1988. (Y4.F76/1:C/13).

692. _____. Committee on Foreign Affairs. <u>The Current
     Crisis in South Africa</u>. 98th Cong., 2nd
     Sess., December 4, 1984. Washington, D.C.:
     G.P.O., 1985. (Y1/4.F76/1:So 8/34).

693. _____. Committee on Foreign Affairs. <u>Internal
     Political Situation in South Africa</u>. 97th
     Cong., 1st Sess., September 14, 1983.
     Washington, D.C.: G.P.O., 1984.
     (Y4.F76/1:P75/8).

694. _____. Committee on Foreign Affairs. Subcommittee
     on Africa. <u>Developments in South Africa:
     United States Policy Responses</u>. 99th Cong.,
     2nd Sess., March 12 1986. Washington, D.C.:
     G.P.O., 1986. 126 pp. (Y4.F76/1:So 8/42).

695. _____. Committee on Foreign Affairs. <u>Oversight of
     the Administration Implementation of the
     Comprehensive Antiapartheid (i.e. Anti-
     Apartheid) Act of 1986 (Public Law 99-440) 2
     and an Assessment of Recent South African
     Political and Economic Developments</u>.
     Hearings Before the Subcommittee on
     International Economic Policy and Trade.

100th Cong., 1st Sess., June 16, 1987.
Washington, D.C.: G.P.O., 1988.
(1/4.F76/1:AN8/6).

696. _____. Committee on Foreign Affairs. Situation in
South Africa: Hearings before the Committee
on Foreign Relations. 99th Cong., 2nd Sess.,
July 22, 23, 24, and 29, 1986. Washington,
D.C.: G.P.O., 1986. (1/4.F76/2:SHRG/99-900).

697. _____. Committee on Foreign Affairs. South Africa
Legislation. 98th Cong., 2nd Sess., April
10, August 1, September 6, 1984. Washington,
D.C.: G.P.O., 1984. (Y4.F76/1:S0 8/33).

698. _____. Committee on Foreign Affairs. Subcommittee
on Africa. Economic Sanctions and Their
Potential Impact on U.S. Corporate
Involvement in South Africa. 99th Cong., 1st
Sess., Washington, D.C.: G.P.O., 1985. 105
pp. (1/4.F76/1:Ec7/16).

699. _____. Committee on Foreign Affairs. Subcommittee
on International Economic Policy and Trade.
The Anti-Apartheid Act of 1985. 99th Cong.,
1st Sess., H.R. 1460. Washington, D.C.:
G.P.O., 1986. 340 pp. (1/4.F76/1:An8/3).

700. _____. Committee on Ways and Means. Anti-
Apartheid Act of 1986: Report Together with
Dissenting and Supplemental Views.
Washington, D.C.: G.P.O., 1986. (Y1.1/8/99-
638. ptl.).

701. _____. Subcommittee on International Economic
Policy and Trade. Controls on Exports to
South Africa. 97th Cong., 2nd Sess.,
February 9, 1982. Washington, D.C.:
Congressional Information Service, 321 pp.
(H381-63).

Looks at the effectiveness of U.S. arms sale
embargo against South Africa in protest of that
country's system of racial separation.

702. _____. Subcommittee on International Economic
        Policy and Trade. U.S. Corporate Activities
        in South Africa. 97th Cong., 1st Sess. H.R.
        3008. May 18, 1982. Washington, D.C.:
        Congressional Information Service, 327 pp.
        (H381-60).

        Examines two bills that are designed to react
        to South Africa's system of racial discrimination.

703. _____. Subcommittee on Human Rights and
        International Organization. Implementation
        of Congressionally Mandated Human Rights
        Provisions. 97th Cong. 1st Sess., March 9,
        17, 1982. Washington, D.C.: Congressional
        Information Service, 224-253, 320-346.
        (H381-6.5).

        Reviews the political situation in African
        countries and examines the U.S. opposition to
        apartheid practices in South Africa.

704. _____. Committee on Ways and Means. Sub-committee
        on Trade. Written Comments on Certain Tariff
        and Trade Bills. Washington, D.C.: G.P.O.,
        1985. 1112 pp. (Y4.W36: WMCP99-11).

705. U.S. Congress. Senate. Committee on
        Appropriations. Sub-committee on the
        District of Columbia. District of Columbia
        Appropriations for Fiscal Year 1986. 99th
        Cong., 1st Sess., S. Hrg. 99-238.
        Washington, D.C.: G.P.O., 1985. 625 pp.

        Covers hearings on the topics of protests and
        demonstrations near the South African embassy.

706. U.S. Congress. Senate. Committee on Banking,
        Housing, and Urban Affairs. The Anti-
        Apartheid Act of 1986. 99th Cong., 2nd
        Sess., S. 2498. July 15, 1986. Washington,
        D.C.: G.P.O., 1986. (Y/4. B22/3: SHRG/99-
        848).

707. _____. Committee on Banking, Housing, and Urban
       Affairs. The Anti-Apartheid Act of 1985:
       Hearings Before the Committee on Banking,
       Housing, and Urban Affairs. 99th Cong., 1st
       Sess., S. 635. April 16, May 24, and June 13,
       1985. Washington, D.C.: G.P.O., 1985. (Y/4.
       B22/3 SHRG 99/148).

708. _____. Committee on Foreign Relations.
       Resolution Regarding the Ban on Political
       Activity in South Africa and the Denial of
       Passports to Certain South Africans: Report
       Together with Additional Views. 100th Cong.,
       1st Sess., Washington, D.C.: G.P.O., 1988.

709. _____. Committee on Foreign Relations. Setting
       U.S. Policy Toward Apartheid; Report Together
       with Additional Views to Accompany S. 2701.
       99th Cong., 2nd Sess., Washington, D.C.:
       G.P.O., 1986. 57 pp. (Y1./5:99-370).

710. _____. Committee on Foreign Relations. U.S.
       Policy Toward South Africa. 99th Cong., 1st
       Sess., S. Hrg. 99-212. Washington, D.C.:
       G.P.O., 1985. 318 pp. (Y/4.F76/1: Un 35/66).

711. U.S. Department of State. Southern Africa: U.S.
       Policy in Brief. Washington, D.C.: The
       Department, 1985. 19 pp.

712. _____. A U.S. Policy Toward South Africa.
       Washington, D.C.: Government Printing Office,
       January 1987. 50 pp.

713. U.S. President (1981-:Reagan). Progress Toward
       Ending the System of Apartheid: Communication
       from the President of the United States
       Transmitting the First Annual Report on the
       Extent to Which Significant Progress Has Been
       Made Toward Ending Apartheid in South Africa,
       Pursuant to 22 U.S.C. 5091 (6). Washington,
       D.C.: G.P.O., 1987. (Y1./1/7-100-109).

8.

ANTI-GOVERNMENT RESISTANCE

Monographs

714. Benson, Mary. <u>Nelson Mandela: The Man and the</u>
     <u>Movement</u>. New York: W.W. Norton & Co., 1986.
     269 pp.

     The author covers interviews held with
     Mandela before his imprisonment, on his published
     writings, and on discussions with his family and
     prisoners released from the prison where he is
     being held.

715. _____. <u>South Africa: The Struggle for a</u>
     <u>Birthright</u>. London: International Defence
     and Aid Fund for Southern Africa, 1985. 314
     pp.

     Benson covers the history of the African
     National Congress.

716. Brewer, John D. "Racial Liberation and the Tactic
     of Terror." Chapter 2 in <u>After Soweto: An</u>
     <u>Unfinished Journey</u>. New York: Clarendon
     Press, 1986.

     The author examines the origins of
     revolutionary terrorism in South Africa and takes
     a look at the role of the ANC in utilizing the
     tactic of terrorism.

717. Carter, Gwendolyn M. Which Way Is South Africa
     Going? Bloomington: Indiana University
     Press, 1980. 162 pp.

     In Chapter 4, Carter looks at the origin of
     black consciousness in South Africa and some of
     the events that led to the formation of the
     various black organizations in that country.

718. A Crime Against Humanity: Questions and Answers on
     Apartheid in South Africa. New York: United
     Nations, 1982.

719. Davies, Robert H. The Struggle for South Africa:
     A Reference Guide to Movements, Organizations
     and Institutions. London: Zed Books, 1984.
     440 pp.

     The author says that "This book is intended
     to be used as a reference guide to the
     organizations, movements, and institutions
     involved in the struggle for South Africa in the
     1980's."

720. Davis, Stephen M. Apartheid's Rebels; Inside
     South Africa's Hidden War. New Haven: Yale
     University Press, 1987. 227 pp.

     Davis examines the politics of the African
     National Congress. Also, he provides an inside
     look at the organized activities carried out by
     this organization.

721. Department of Public Information. Combating
     Racial Discrimination. New York: United
     Nations, 1985.

722. Dorabji, Elena V. "South African National
     Congress." Thesis. University of
     California, Berkeley, 1979.

     The author studies the changes of the ANC
     from a non-violent organization to that of a
     guerilla organization.

723. Essack, Karrim. <u>Reform or Revolution in South Africa</u>. Dar es Salaam: Thakers Limited, 1982. 140 pp.

     The author contends that black South Africans are faced with several problems in their fight to end apartheid.

724. Falton, Robert. <u>Black Consciousness in South Africa: The Dialectics of Ideological Resistance to White Supremacy</u>. Albany: State University of New York Press, 1986. 189 pp.

725. Frederikse, Julie. <u>South Africa: A Different Kind of War</u>. Boston: Beacon Press, 1986. 192 pp.

     The author tries to differentiate between the various patterns of resistance that exist in South Africa.

725a. Hanlon, Joseph. <u>Beggar Your Neighbours: Apartheid Power in Southern Africa</u>. Bloomington: Indiana University Press, 1986. 352 pp.

     In Chapter 3, the author examines the role of the African National Congress and how the government is trying to push them out of all states in the region.

726. Harrison, Nancy. <u>Winnie Mandela</u>. New York: G. Braziller, 1986. 183 pp.

     Harrison conveys the reasons for black resistance to apartheid.

727. Harsch, Ernest. <u>South Africa: White Rule, Black Revolts</u>. New York: Pathfinder Press, 1980. 352 pp.

     In chapters 16 and 18, Harsch examines the origins of the black nationalist movement in South Africa and the various groups that were formed through this movement.

728. Herbstein, Denis. <u>White Man, We Want to Talk to</u>
     <u>You</u>. New York: Africana Pub., 1979. 270 pp.

     Herbstein studies the incidents of the riots
in Soweto.

729. Hirson, Baruch. <u>Year of Fire, Year of Ash; The</u>
     <u>Soweto Revolt, Roots of a Revolution</u>. New
     York: Monthly Rev. Press, 1979. 348 pp.

     The author attempts to describe the events
that took place during and after the Soweto
revolt.

730. <u>I Am Prepared to Die</u>. New York: International
     Defense Aid Fund, May 1979. 48 pp.

     Presents excerpts from the court records of
Nelson Mandela's trial in 1962 and the statement
he made from the dock in the 1963 trial for
sedition.

731. <u>International Convention on the Suppression and</u>
     <u>Punishment of the Crime of Apartheid</u>. New
     York: United Nations Centre Against
     Apartheid, May 1982. 9pp.

732. International Defense and Aid Fund for Southern
     Africa. <u>One Union's Fight Against Apartheid -</u>
     <u>The Story of the Free Dave Kitson Campaign</u>.
     London: 1980.

732a. James, Wilmot G., ed. <u>The State of Apartheid</u>.
     Boulder: Lynne Rienner Publishers, 1987.
     210 pp.

     In Chapter 4, the author talks about the
state of emergency and urban disorder in South
Africa.

733. Kane-Berman, J. <u>Soweto: Black Revolt White</u>
     <u>Reaction.</u> Athens, Ohio: Ohio University
     Press, 1981. 268 pp.

734. Lapping, Brian. <u>Apartheid: A History</u>. New York: G. Braziller, 1986.

The author observes the ANC, PAC, UDF, and several other groups intent on bringing an end to the system of apartheid.

735. Magapatona, Patrick. "The Role of Transnational Corporations, Foreign Investments and the National Bourgeoisie in South Africa." Paper presented by the African National Congress of South Africa to the 2nd Congress of the Association of Third World Economists, held in Havana, Cuba, April 26-30th, 1981.

736. Meltzer, Milton. <u>Winnie Mandela: The Soul of South Africa</u>. New York: Viking Kestrel, 1986. 54 pp.

Covers the life and civil rights work of this South African leader.

737. Motlhabi, Mokgethi B.G. <u>The Theory and Practice of Black Resistance to Apartheid: A Social-Ethical Analysis</u>. Johannesburg: Skotaville Publishers, 1984.

738. Mzimela, Sipo E. <u>Apartheid: South African Nazism</u>. New York: Vantage, 1983. 245 pp.

In chapter 10, the author examines the rise of the black resistance movement in South Africa and their struggle to bring an end to apartheid.

739. Nkomo, Mokubung O. <u>Student Culture and Activism in Black South African Universities: The Roots of Resistance</u>. Westport: Greenwood Press, 1982. 209 pp.

Nkomo examines the basic concept of student culture and radicalism in African universities in South Africa. Moreover, the author attempts to find out to what extent have Bantu education and other events affected students' resistance to the system of apartheid.

740. North, James. <u>Freedom Rising</u>. New York: North
         American Library, 1986.

         North talks with various people in Southern
     Africa, about the liberation of blacks and the
     dismantling of apartheid.

741. Pheko, Motsoko. <u>Apartheid: The Story of a
         Dispossessed People</u>. London: Marram Bks.,
         1984. 196 pp.

         The author attempts to describe the struggle
     of blacks in South Africa from the early days
     through the present.

742. Pomeroy, William J. <u>Apartheid, Imperialism, and
         African Freedom</u>. New York: International
         Publishers, 1986. 259 pp.

743. <u>Repression in a Time of 'Reform': A Look at Events
         in the Transvaal Since August, 1984</u>.
         Johannesburg: United Democratic Front, 1974.
         38 pp.

744. Saul, John S. <u>The Crisis in South Africa: Class
         Defense, Class Revolution</u>. New York: Monthly
         Review Press, 1981. 156 pp.

         Saul seeks to describe the backdrop for
     revolution in South Africa. He talks about the
     role of the ANC and what they hope to accomplish.

745. <u>South Africa 1984: Renewed Resistance, Increased
         Repression</u>. Washington: Lawyers' Committee
         for Civil Rights Under Law, 1985. 47 pp.

746. <u>South Africa: Time of Agony, Time of Destiny; The
         Upsurge of Popular Protest</u>. New York:
         Methuen, Inc., 1987. 496 pp.

         Looks at the inception and make-up of the
     black organizations and their fight to end
     apartheid. Also, examines the July 1985 state of
     emergency that was imposed by the government.

747. <u>Talking With the ANC</u>. Pretoria, Africa: Bureau
        for Information, 1986. 42 pp.

        Provides an overview of the ANC and their
    relations with the Soviet Union. It also examines
    their policies on negotiations and violence.

748. Tambo, O.R. "Attack Advance, Give the Enemy No
        Quarter." Message of the National Executive
        Committee of the African National Congress on
        the occasion of January 8, 1986.

749. _____. "Render South Africa Ungovernable."
        Message of the National Executive Committee
        of the African National Congress on the
        occasion of January 8, 1985.

750. Tatum, Lyle, ed. <u>South Africa, Challenge and
        Hope</u>. New York: Hill and Wang, Inc., 1987.

751. <u>Twentieth Anniversary of the Founding of SWAPO,
        1960-1980</u>: Luanda, Angola: Central Committee
        of SWAPO, 1980. 17 pp.

752. <u>Unity in Action: A Photographic History of the
        African National Congress, South Africa,
        1912-1982</u>. London: The Congress, 1982. 156
        pp.

753. Voorhes, Meg. <u>The Modernization of Apartheid</u>.
        Washington: Investor Responsibility Research
        Center, 1982. 46 pp.

754. Wilmot, Patrick F. <u>Apartheid and African
        Liberation: The Grief and the Hope, Ile-Ife,
        Nigeria</u>: University of Ife Press, 1980. 194
        pp.

Articles

755. "ANC Refugees Leave Lesotho." <u>South Africa R</u> 1:
        31 (September 16, 1983): 8-9.

756. "The Anti-Racist Resistance Movement Intensifies."
     Intl Affairs (May 1985): 133-135.

     Covers an interview with Alfred Nzo,
     secretary-general of the ANC, regarding his views
     on the current war against the South African
     government.

757. "Arrests Mount as Campus Anti-Apartheid Demos
     Spread." Times Higher Educ Suppl No. 654
     (May 17, 1985): 10.

757a. Bilski, Andrew. "The Religious Revolt Against
     Apartheid." Macl Mag 101 (March 14, 1988):
     38.

758. "Black Rage, White Fist." Time (August 5, 1985):
     24-32.

     Covers the events that led to the
     government's state of emergency and the
     international community's reaction to those
     events.

759. "Black Students in South Africa Reported
     Increasingly Restive over Racial Policies."
     Chron Higher Educ 23 (November 11, 1981): 19.

     The South African Institute of Race Relations
     reported that there was an increase in student
     dissatisfaction among black secondary school
     students and university students. The
     dissatisfaction stemmed from the inequality in the
     education system.

760. Buthelezi, Mangosuthu G. "Anti-Apartheid: Without
     a Secret Agenda." Midstream 33 (June/July
     1987): 6-8.

     Buthelezi elaborates on violence and just how
     far the black South African will be pushed before
     using violence as a means to bring an end to
     apartheid.

761. Calabrese, Mike, and Kendall, Mike.   "The Black
       Agenda for South Africa."   Nation 241
       (October 26, 1985): 393+.

       The authors examine the continuous growth of
       the ANC and the black unions in South Africa.
       Also, they contend that the violence of the ANC
       and the economic position of the unions are
       essential tools in bringing an end to apartheid.

762. Campbell, Keith.   "Prospects for Terrorism in
       South Africa."   South Africa Intl 14: 2
       (October 1983): 397-417.

763. Charney, C.   "Second University Closed as Student
       Unrest Continues."   Times Higher Educ Suppl
       No. 556 (July 1, 1983): 7.

       The author reveals that the University of the
       North was closed following clashes with students.
       The conflict resulted in a commemorative meeting
       observing the anniversary of the Soweto uprising.

764. _____.   "Thinking of Revolution: The New South
       African Intelligentsia."   Mo R 38 (December
       1986): 10-19.

765. Cowell, Alan.   "Defiance in South Africa."   NY
       Times M (April 14, 1985): 30-36+.

       The author explores the rise of a new
       resistance movement.

766. Dadoo, Yusuf.   "Crisis of the Racist System in the
       South of Africa."   World Marxist R 26
       (December 1982): 18-25.

       The chairman of South Africa's Communist
       party expresses his views on the political and
       ideological crisis in South Africa. He also makes
       mention of the various groups in that country who
       oppose the system of apartheid.

767. Davis, Jennifer. "The Illusion of Reform, the
        Reality of Resistance: 1984 in South Africa."
        Chr & Crisis 45 (February 4/18, 1985): 8-13.

        Davis says, "The South African regime still
has massive resources, and the support of major
foreign corporations and powerful Western leaders
like Margaret Thatcher and Ronald Reagan. All
these may help hold the structure together for a
while, but in the end the walls of apartheid will
not stand against the force of the cyclone."

768. Dempster, C. "Black Students Clash with Police."
        Times Higher Educ Suppl. No. 568 (September
        23, 1983): 6

        Dempster examines the demonstrations and
unrest by black students at two of South Africa's
largest ethnic universities.

769. _____. "Laying the Explosive Charge." Times
        Higher Educ Suppl No. 625 (October 26, 1984):
        9.

        Dempster examines the statements made by a
political science professor on the growing despair
and resentment of black students in South Africa.

770. _____. "Lecture Boycott Accompanies Riots."
        Times Higher Educ Suppl no. 619 (September
        14, 1984): 8.

        The author examines the reasons why the black
students at the University of the North have
decided to boycott their classes.

771. _____. "Police Clash with Black Students." Times
        Higher Educ Suppl no. 620 (September 21,
        1984): 10.

        Dempster observes the various protests,
boycotts, marches, and violence that took place
commemorating the anniversary of the death of
black consciousness leader Steve Biko.

772. _____. "South Africa Stands by Separatist
         Policy." <u>Times Higher Educ Suppl</u> no. 578
         (December 2, 1983): 9.

         The author examines the responses of the De
    Lange Report on education in South Africa.

773. _____. "Violence at Peace Demo." <u>Times Higher
         Educ Suppl</u> no. 667 (August 16, 1985): 1.

         Dempster details the demonstration by
    students at the University of the Witwatersrand
    and the police confrontation that ensued, all
    resulting because of the state of emergency act.

774. Douglis, Carole A.,and Davis, Stephen M. "Revolt
         on the Veldt." <u>Harper</u> 267 (December, 1983):
         30-41.

775. El-Khawas, Mohamed A. "The Liberation Struggle in
         South Africa: Will the 1980's Be Decisive?"
         <u>Trans Afr Forum</u> 2 (Fall 1983): 79-91.

         The author examines the resurgence of the
    African National Congress and its role in the
    struggle to bring an end to apartheid.

776. Everett, Richard. "South Africa: Breaking Out of
         the Cocoon." <u>Africa Rep</u> 32
         (September/October 1987): 31-34.

         Everett alludes to a meeting held by members
    of the ANC and liberal white South Africans
    concerning the system of apartheid.

777. F.,M. "Koeberg Blast: Guerrillas Hit South Africa
         Nuke." <u>So Africa</u> 16 (January-February 1983):
         21.

778. "Few Safe Havens for Apartheid's Exiles." <u>Africa
         Rep</u> 29 (January/February 1984): 14-17.

         Examines the government of South Africa's
    Policy toward neighboring countries that harbor
    South African refugees.

779. Fitzgerald, Mary Anne. "The OAU: A New Military."
        Africa Rep 31 (September/October 1986): 66-
        69.

        The author studies the Organization of
African Unity and the methods it uses to dismantle
apartheid.

780. "Four Voices of Unease in South Africa: Candid
        First-Person Accounts Provide a Striking
        Picture of Racial Tensions Gripping the Last
        White-Ruled Nation South of the Sahara;
        Blacks, Whites and Coloureds All Are Braced
        for Trouble." US News World Rep 91
        (September 7, 1981): 35-37+.

781. Francis, Samuel T. "Communism, Terrorism, and the
        African National Congress." J Soc and Pol
        Econ Stud 11 (Spring 1986): 55-71.

        The author covers the origin of the ANC and
its relationship with the South African Communist
Party. Moreover, he gives examples of the ANC's
tactics and how it relates to Leninist ideology.

781a. Getz, Arlene. "Only Free Men Can Negotiate:
        Nelson Mandela Hospitalized." Newsweek 112
        (August 29, 1988): 37.

782. Greene, E. "Students Plan Campus Protests Against
        Apartheid." Chron Higher Educ 31 (October 9,
        1985): 32.

        Greene observes the various U.S. groups'
plans for demonstrations on more than 100 colleges
and universities for the first National Anti-
Apartheid Protest Day.

783. Grundy, Kenneth W. "Race Politics in South
        Africa: Change and Revolt." Curr Hist 85
        (May 1986): 197-200+.

        Grundy examines the government's use of
apartheid as a means of ending black unrest in
South Africa.

784. Haigh, Bruce. "The Black Consciousness Movement in South Africa." <u>Aust Out</u> 35 (August 1981): 169-180.

785. Harsch, Ernest. "South Africa: Black Workers Stand Up to Apartheid Regime; ANC Challenges Apartheid Regime; Repression vs. Mass Radicalization." <u>Inter Pr</u> (July 11, 1983): 376-380.

786. _____. "South Africa: Botha Proclaims, 'State of Emergency'; Continued Black Protests Defy Police Troops." <u>Inter Pr</u> 23 (August 19, 1985): 484-485.

Harsch touches upon the various protests and demonstrations in South Africa that led to the state of emergency.

787. _____. "South Africa: More Whites Reject Apartheid; Join UDF, Campaign Against Military Conscription." <u>Inter Pr</u> 24 (May 19, 1986): 308-309.

788. _____. "South Africa: New Stage in the Revolutionary Struggle; Racist Apartheid System Shaken to Its Roots." <u>Inter Pr</u> 23 (September 23, 1985): 548-553.

The author explores the role of the UDF and the ANC and the unionization among black workers in South Africa.

789. _____. "South Africa: Pretoria Readjusts Shackles on Blacks; Drops Old Pass Books, Prepares New Apartheid Controls." <u>Inter Pr</u> 24 (June 2, 1986): 346-349.

790. Hasting, Adrian. "The Christian Churches and Liberation Movements in Southern Africa." <u>Afric Affairs</u> 80:320 (July 1981): 345-354.

791. Heaven, Patrick, and Stones, Chris. "Attitudes Toward a South African Liberation Movement." <u>J Confl Res</u> 30 (September 1986): 487-496.

          Investigates the attitudes toward the ANC
     among black and white South African university
     students.

792. Hovey, Gail. "Human Rights Violations in
          Apartheid South Africa." <u>Soc Sci Rec</u> 22:2
          (Fall 1985): 9-12.

          Hovey reveals that the political resistance
     toward apartheid in South Africa is constantly
     growing and government repression continues to
     grow as well.

793. Iyer, Pico. "The Fires of Anger." <u>Time</u> 125
          (April 8, 1985): 40-41+.

          Iyer describes some of the violence that has
     taken place by blacks in protest of the
     government's restraints.

794. "Journals Foresee Rise in ANC Actions." <u>Afr News</u>
          (February 16, 1984): 3-6.

          This article observes the support by blacks
     of the ANC and how the ANC is causing problems for
     the South African Government.

795. Knight, Robin. "Rumblings of Race War in South
          Africa: In City and Countryside, Whites Are
          Bracing To Meet the Black Challenge; As
          Tensions Rise, Full-Scale Conflict Seems
          Inevitable." <u>US News World Rep</u> 88 (March 17,
          1980): 43-44.

796. Lodge, Tom. "The African National Congress,
          1982." <u>South Africa R</u> 1 (1983): 50-54.

797. Lodge, Tom, and Swilling, Mark. "The Year of the
          Amabuthu." <u>Africa Rep</u> 31 (March/April
          1986):4.

          Lodge examines the role of the children of
     South Africa in the resistance fight against the
     government. Also, the author explores the

negative aspects of involving children in guerilla warfare.

798. "Making South Africa Ungovernable." Black Sch 15 (November/December 1984): 2-14.

This interview with David Ndaba, administrative secretary of the African National Congress, reveals the ANC's strategy for the 1980's and its fight to end apartheid in South Africa.

799. Mothhabi, Mokgethi. "The Theory and Practice of Black Resistance to Apartheid: A Social-Ethical Analysis of the Internal Struggle for Political and Social Change in South Africa, 1948-1978." Boston University Graduate School, DAI, 1980, 41: 2170-A.

This work analyzes the resistance activities of three South African groups, the ANC, PAC, and BCM. Also, it examines the practices and ideologies of these organizations.

800. Mufson, Steven. "Who Is the ANC?" New Repub 195 (August 25, 1986): 20-22+.

Mufson talks about the mystique and the growing power of the ANC.

801. "New Mood, New Factors in Struggle for South Africa." Chr and Crisis 40 (August 18, 1980): 22-28.

802. Nkomo, Joshua. "The Struggle Until Victory." R Intl Affairs 30 (February 5, 1979): 67.

The President of ZAPU discusses the reasons why the countries of Zimbabwe, Namibia, and South Africa are still the strongholds of racism and colonialism and why his groups and others are constantly trying to bring an end to those systems.

803. Nzo, Alfred. "Stepping Up the Fight Against the
        Racist Enemy." World Marxist R 26: 9
        (September 1983): 20-26.

        Nzo says that the African National Congress
        has declared 1982 the "Year of Unity in Action,"
        and asks the entire continent of Africa to get
        involved in the fight to end apartheid in South
        Africa.

804. "Oliver Tambo: We Are Committed Interna-
        tionalists." New Times (January 1980): 22-
        23.

        The President of the ANC talks about its
        alliance with Zimbabwe and the racial problems in
        South Africa.

805. O'Meara, Patrick. "South Africa: The Politics of
        Change." Curr Hist 80: 464 (March 1981):
        111-114, 134.

        O'Meara discusses the problems that face the
        South African government in the 1980's, especially
        young black South Africans.

806. Pleming, Susan. "Hundreds of Students Held in
        South Africa." Times Higher Educ Suppl no.
        668 (August 23, 1985): 7.

        Pleming reports that many of the students
        being held under the government's state of
        emergency regulation are rank and file
        members of the Congress of South African students,
        and other youth groups.

807. Pokrovsky, A. "The Apartheid Regime and Its
        Imperialist Patrons." Intl Affairs no. 9
        (September 1986): 101-105, 160.

        The author looks at the government, foreign
        affairs and resistance being waged against
        apartheid in South Africa.

808. Rich, Paul B. "Insurgency, Terrorism and the
     Apartheid System in South Africa." Pol Stud
     32 (1984): 68-85.

     Rich elaborates on the increasing development
of guerrilla activities in South Africa and the
government's response to this problem.

809. Rieder, Eric. "Crucibles of the Black Rebellion."
     Nation 241 (September 7, 1985): 169-172.

     This article observes the rise and spread of
black protest following Botha's announcement of a
state of emergency.

810. Smith, William E. "Black Rage, White Fist." Time
     (August 5, 1985): 24-32.

     Smith discusses the events that took place in
South Africa following the enforcement of the
state of emergency act.

811. "South Africa." Africa Rep 31 (March-April 1986):
     4-36.

     Explains the emergence of children as major
participants in the fight against the South
African government.

812. "South Africa." Progressive 49 (February 1985):
     18, 20-24.

     The momentum for resistance to apartheid
among blacks is gathering day by day.

813. "South Africa: More Whites Reject Apartheid; Join
     UDF, Campaign Against Military Conscription."
     Inter Pr 24 (May 19, 1986): 308-309.

814. "South Africa's Civil War." Newsweek 107 (June
     23, 1986): 34-43.

     This article covers the reaction of blacks in
South Africa following Botha's renewed tactic of
instituting the state of emergency act.

815. Streek, Barry. "Black Strategies Against
     Apartheid." <u>Africa Rep</u> 25 (July/August
     1980): 35-39.

     The author examines the various tactics used
by black groups in South Africa who are trying to
bring an end to apartheid.

816. Tambo, Oliver. "Oliver Tambo: President of the
     African National Congress of South Africa."
     <u>Africa Rep</u> 26:5 (September-October 1981): 20-
     22.

     The president contends that the ANC would
like to see people of the U.S. look at the
practical ways to isolate the apartheid government
and support the ANC.

817. _____. "Speech by ANC Leader Oliver Tambo:
     Perspectives for the Revolutionary Struggle
     Against Apartheid (Address by the President
     of the African National Congress)." <u>Inter Pr</u>
     23 (March 4, 1985): 116-121.

818. _____. "We Are Determined to Liberate
     Ourselves." <u>Inter Pr</u> 24 (February 24, 1986):
     100-105.

     Tambo talks about the tasks facing the
African National Congress and their fight to end
apartheid.

819. "Ten Years After Soweto: Apartheid Under Siege."
     <u>Polit Aff</u> 65 (July 1986): 3-7.

     Covers an interview with Alfred Nzo, one of
the main leaders of the African National Congress.

820. "Tensions in Southern Africa: What Lies Ahead."
     <u>To the Point</u> 8 (January 5, 1979): 69.

821. "The UDF: Resurgence of Resistance." <u>Africa Rep</u>
     29 (January/February 1984): 48-50.

Studies the activities and tactics of the
United Democratic Front fight against the racial
policies of the government of South Africa.

822. Villa-Vicencio, Charles. "Twenty-Five Years After
     Sharpeville." Africa Rep 30 (May-June 1985):
     63-67.

Contends that there are very few options left
to anti-apartheid groups in their quest to
dismantle South Africa's government.

823. Whitaker, Mark. "Mandela: Battling Apartheid's
     Rule." Newsweek 106 (December 16, 1985): 34-
     36.

Whitaker comments on Mandela's defiance of
the government of South Africa and her continued
struggle to bring an end to apartheid.

824. Zille, H. "Bitter Ideological Dispute in South
     Africa Splits 2 Major Groups of Black
     Students." Chron Higher Educ 30 (May 15,
     1985): 1+.

The author examines the division in the two
major black student groups--the United Democratic
and the Azanian People's Organization--and what
can be done to bring an end to this dispute.

825. _____. "Black Students Clash with South African
     Police at U. of the North; Campus Protest
     Reassessed." Chron Higher Educ 31 (September
     25, 1985): 39.

826. _____. "Black Students Have Become a Prime Target
     During South Africa's State of Emergency."
     Chron Higher Educ 30 (August 7, 1985): 1+.

The author examines the government's
crackdown on black students and other young people
after the institution of the State of Emergency
Act.

827. _____. "Dissident Groups in South Africa Fear
Arrests Signal a Major Crackdown by
Government." Chron Higher Educ 29 (November
28, 1984): 39-40.

Zille states that "students and labor leaders
say there is a carefully orchestrated campaign by
senior government spokesmen to characterize their
organizations as subversive."

828. _____. "First in South Africa: Afrikaner Students
Form an Organization to Oppose Apartheid."
Chron Higher Educ 21 (January 19, 1981): 15-
16.

Zille talks about the formation of a small
group of liberal Afrikaan-speaking students'
organization, which seeks to form a political
organization open to all races.

829. _____. "Low-Level Civil War Being Waged in South
Africa, Observers Say; Students in Forefront
of Protests." Chron Higher Educ 30 (April 3,
1985): 33-34.

Zille recounts some of the clashes (and
killings) that have taken place between students
and the government of South Africa since September.

830. _____. "9 Afrikaner Student Leaders Prevented
From Going to Anti-Apartheid Meeting." Chron
Higher Educ 31 (October 23, 1985): 35+.

The author indicates that the government
withdrew their passports after they refused to
cancel their meeting with the Youth League of the
banned African National Congress.

831. _____. "South Africa Gags Student Newspapers in
Effort to Silence Apartheid Foes." Chron
Higher Educ 26 (July 6, 1983): 15.

The author reveals that the government has
decided to invoke a new method of silencing

student newspapers that have spoken out against apartheid.

832. _____. "South Africa Gags 2 Student Journalists, Bans Their Anti-Apartheid Newspaper." Chron Higher Educ 24 (April 28, 1982): 15.

Two students at the University of the Witwatersrand and a research officer were banned because their newspaper, the National, was considered to be critical of the government's policies.

833. _____. "South Africa Moves to Silence Students Opposing Apartheid." Chron Higher Educ 22 (July 6, 1981): 13.

The author reveals that the government has decided to ban two of the leaders of the student organizations opposing apartheid.

834. _____. "South Africa Widens State of Emergency; Students and Faculty Members Detained." Chron Higher Educ 31 (November 6, 1985): 1+.

The author confirms that the South African government extended its state of emergency to the Western Cape region where numerous students were detained.

835. _____. "South African Campuses Explode in Protest of Government Policies." Chron Higher Educ 31 (September 4, 1985): 81+.

Zille contends that a large majority of white students have joined with black students in opposing the actions of the government's apartheid policies.

836. _____. "20 Detained, Several Injured as Police Storm Campus Protest in South Africa." Chron Higher Educ 31 (September 18, 1985): 39-40.

Documents

837. U.N. General Assembly. A/AC. 115/L.531. Letter
     Dated 29 July 1980. Addressed to the
     Chairman of the Special Committee Against
     Apartheid from the President of the African
     National Congress, Issued in Accordance with
     the Decision Taken by the Special Committee
     at Its 460th Meeting Held on 11 September
     1980 - 15 September 1980. 2 pp.

838. _____. A/AC. 115/L.547. International Seminar
     on the Implementation and Reinforcement of
     the Arms Embargo Against South Africa, 1-3
     April 1981. Report of the World Campaign
     Against Military and Nuclear Collaboration
     with South Africa 8 May 1981. 36 pp.

839. _____. A/AC.115/L.550. International Day of
     Solidarity with the Struggle of Women of
     South Africa and Namibia. Messages Issued in
     Accordance with the Decision Taken by the
     Special Committee at Its 479th Meeting Held
     on 11 August 1981-27 August 1981. 8 pp.

840. _____. A/AC.115/L.559. Messages Received on the
     Day of Solidarity with South African
     Political Prisoners. 23 October 1981. 6 pp.

841. _____. A/AC. 115/L.563. Statement by Oliver
     Tambo, President of the African National
     Congress on 12 January 1982. Issued in
     Accordance with the Decision Taken by the
     Special Committee Against Apartheid at Its
     489th Meeting Held on 12 January 1982-25
     January 1982. 6 pp.

842. _____. A/AC.115/L.572. Messages Received on the
     International Day of Solidarity with the
     Struggling People of South Africa, Soweto
     Day, 16 June 1982. 10 pp.

843. _____. A/Conf. 94/5. The Role of Women in the
     Struggle for Liberation in Zimbabwe, Namibia
     and South Africa: Report of the Secretary-
     General, 1980. 38 pp.

APPENDIX

ECONOMIC AND LABOR CONDITIONS:

1). The Bantu Laws Amendment Act of 1970 - amendment
    of the 1964 labor act which gave the Minister
    the right to prohibit the work of Africans in
    specific classes of trade or employment and
    in specific areas.

2). Black Labour Relations Regulation Act 1977 - which
    basically sought to exclude all Africans from
    becoming members of registered trade unions.

3). The Factories, Machinery, and Building Work Act -
    passed in 1941, later amended in 1960, gave
    the President the power to make regulations
    regarding the division or separation in any
    workplace of people different classes, races,
    or sexes.

4). The Mines and Works Acts - prohibits blacks from
    working in skilled positions.

5). Plural Relations and Development act, No. 98 of
    1979 - fines the employer who is found guilty
    of employing blacks that do not have a permit
    to work in a particular area.

EDUCATION:

1). <u>Bantu Education Act</u> - empowers the Minister of
    Education to direct and establish schools in
    urban black townships, rural areas, and black
    areas not already having self-government.

2). <u>Universities Amendment Act, Number 85 of 1983</u> -
    gives the Minister of Education the power to
    establish quotas for students allowed to
    attend institutions of higher learning
    established for racial groups.

SOCIAL CONDITIONS:

1). <u>Group Areas Act</u> - gave the government of South
    Africa control over the occupation and
    ownership of property and buildings
    throughout that country. Excluded were black
    homelands and townships and coloured
    reserves.

2). <u>Native Laws Amendment Act</u> - states that any native
    born a black South African could visit an
    urban area for up to 72 hours without
    obtaining a special permit.

3). <u>Nursing Act</u> - provides that all nurses, midwives,
    and student midwives and nurses should be
    members of a common Nursing Association.
    However, separate branches should be
    established for each race.

4). <u>Prevention of Illegal Squatting Act</u> - states no
    citizen might enter any building or property
    without lawful reason or without the
    permission of the owner or lawful occupier.

5). <u>Railways and Harbours Act</u> - provided that the
    government reserve the right to authorize
    accommodation on trains for the sole use of
    persons belonging to a particular class or
    race.

6). <u>Reservations of Separate Amenities Act of 1953</u> -
     gives the government the power to restrict
     public facilities or reserve these areas to a
     particular racial group.

GOVERNMENT:

1). <u>Criminal Law Amendment Act</u> - under this act the
     Postmaster-General could open any postal
     material suspected of containing money or
     other items intended to aid campaigns of
     protest or demonstration against the
     government.

2). <u>Gatherings and Demonstrations Act</u> - gives the
     government the authority to ban any
     demonstrations or marches in the area of
     Parliament in Cape Town.

3). <u>Indemnity Act</u> - indicates that no criminal or
     civil proceedings can be brought against the
     government or any of its officers in respect
     to any actions taken by the government to
     quell internal disorder.

4). <u>Natives Acts, No. 67</u> - gives an official
     the authority to order a black to produce a
     pass book at any time.

5). <u>Proclamation R 268 of 1968</u> - this law made it an
     offense in South Africa, except with official
     permission, to address any gathering or
     preside in a black area at which there were
     more than 10 blacks present.

6). <u>Riotous Assemblies Act</u> - makes it an offense for
     those that are assembling or promoting people
     to attend a meeting that was already declared
     illegal by the government.

7). Second General Law Amendment Act, No. 94 - states
     that any person who verbally abuses or
     performs any act that might cause or ferment
     feelings of hostile actions between the
     different races of the country shall be found
     guilty.

8). Suppression of Communism Act - allows for the
     government to investigate any individual or
     organization that might be considered
     adhering to the objectives of communism.

9). Urban Areas Consolidation Act - Section 29 of this
     act says that undesirable blacks, mainly
     those that have been unemployed or did not
     maintain steady employment, may be sent to a
     prison farm for up to two years.

AUTHOR INDEX

SUBJECT INDEX

Y